Overcoming Hurtful Words opens a very important conversation about the power of your words and how you've been wounded by others. The nine practices Janell Rardon outlines will empower you to let go of any negative narratives so that you can gain a healthy sense of self and the communication skills you need for a rich, meaningful life.

Georgia Shaffer, M.A., psychologist, professional life coach, author of *Taking Out Your Emotional Trash*

In *Overcoming Hurtful Words*, Janelle Rardon does more than help us get over words that wound; she teaches us to actually rewrite the stories of who we are with a God who loves us and sees beyond those words to the truth of who we are.

Kathi Lipp, best-selling author of *Overwhelmed*

Despite the pain of past wounds (words), the heart has an expansive "capacity and potential to live out it's God-breathed purpose." YOU too can share in this amazing testimony of a life story re-written!

Daphne Delay, author of *Facing the Mirror, Facing God, and Facing the Enemy*

In *Overcoming Hurtful Words,* Janell Rardon shows firsthand how love transforms hurt and woundedness into hope and healing. Read these words and let this process encourage you to find new joy in your life!

Rosemary **Trible**, author of *Fear 2 Freedom,* founder of Fear 2 Freedom (F2F)

Janell's deep faith and her passion for helping others heal is evident in her book, *Overcoming Hurtful Words*. She beautifully integrates Scripture with the tools of reflection, reframing, and re-authoring hurtful words as she guides us on a transformational path to freedom.

Becky VanValin, MSW, counselor, author, international speaker

Overcoming Hurtful Words is full of Christian-based guidance for how to turn a negative narrative of experiences into a Christ-guided positive destiny. This book is a powerful tool, indeed!

Dr. Antipas L. Harris, president of
the Urban Renewal Center

Author Janell Rardon shares practical steps, grounded in biblical truth. This is a book you'll return to again and again.

Edie Melson, award-winning author of
While My Child Is Away

Janell's writing style creates an environment where the reader feels loved and supported through the process of examining hurtful situations. As a pastor, I know this book will help so many women on the journey of healing.

Rev. Stephanie Parker, New Creation United Methodist Church,
Chesapeake, Virginia

Overcoming Hurtful Words helps wounded people reconstruct the negative narratives of their lives. Be ready to soar on wings like eagles!

Pastor Jim and Sheryl Wood,
First Presbyterian Church of Norfolk

Overcoming Hurtful Words is a symphony of passion and practicality, encouraging and equipping women to move beyond the hurts of the past to transform their lives through the power of Scripture.

Rev. Valena Hoy, Associate Pastor, First Presbyterian Church,
Norfolk, Virginia

OVERCOMING
hurtful
WORDS

OVERCOMING
hurtful
WORDS

Rewrite Your Own Story

JANELL RARDON

WORTHY®
Inspired

Published by Worthy Inspired, an imprint of Worthy Publishing Group, a division of Worthy Media, Inc.,
One Franklin Park, 6100 Tower Circle, Suite 210, Franklin, TN 37067.

WORTHY is a registered trademark of Worthy Media, Inc.

Helping people experience the heart of God.

Library of Congress Cataloging-in-Publication Data

Names: Rardon, Janell, author.
Title: Overcoming hurtful words : rewrite your own story / Janell Rardon.
Description: Franklin, TN : Worthy Inspired, 2017.
Identifiers: LCCN 2017034912 | ISBN 9781683970507 (paperback)
Subjects: LCSH: Christian life. | Healing--Religious aspects--Christianity. |
  Self-esteem--Religious aspects--Christianity. |
  Self-realization--Religious aspects--Christianity. | BISAC: RELIGION /
  Christian Life / Personal Growth. | SELF-HELP / Personal Growth /
  Self-Esteem.
Classification: LCC BV4501.3 .R37 2017 | DDC 248.8/6--dc23
LC record available at https://lccn.loc.gov/2017034912

*Author's Note: I have tried to recreate events, locales, and conversations from my memories of them. To
maintain their anonymity, in some instances I have changed the names of individuals and places. I may have
also changed some identifying characteristics and details such as physical properties, occupations, and places
of residence.

ISBN: 978-1-68397-050-7

Hearts, Grudge, and Love graphics designed: Terri Podlenski, MA | SmartCreativeLab.com
Cover design Bruce Gore | GoreStudio.com
Cover art: Shutterstock, iStock
Page layout: Bart Dawson

Printed in the United States of America
17 18 19 20 21 22 lbm 10 9 8 7 6 5 4 3 2 1

Dedicated to the love of my life, Rob—and to one of our favorite places on earth, the Outer Banks of North Carolina (OBX).

So long ago, while floating on a surfboard, we dreamed of a life together. We could not have known at the time what God had in mind. While beachcombing, building sandcastles, and braving Jockey's Ridge, we raised three of the most remarkable children—Candace, Brooke, and Grant. Waves have crashed against our little family, yet we have weathered the storms and come through stronger, wiser, and healthier.

When I was caught in the riptide of my crushing heartrift, your strong hand saved me. If the sand dunes of our heartlifting two-hundred-mile coastline could tell our story, they would say, "Many waters cannot quench love, nor can rivers drown it" (Song of Solomon 8:7 NLT).

May our story—because this truly is *our story*—guide others to the Light; like our beloved Cape Hatteras lighthouse, may it lead them to the shores of safety and serenity.

"Do not fear [anything], for I am with you;
Do not be afraid, for I am your God.
I will strengthen you, be assured I will help you;
I will certainly take hold of you
with My righteous right hand [a hand of justice,
of power, of victory, of salvation]."
Isaiah 41:10 (AMP)

CONTENTS

Part Three: Reauthor
Future Freedom: Will I Ever Trust Again?

GLOSSARY

Fault line: a past hurt.

Fracture: a present pain.

Heartlift: the process of vocalizing crushing pain in a healthy manner that brings closure, emotional healing, and lasting freedom.

Heartrift: deep wounds caused by heartbreaking words from close, trusted friends and family members.

Heartshift: that moment in time when the heart awakens to truth.

Heartsift: taking necessary time to examine past behaviors/communication skills (or the history of hurts) thoroughly to isolate those that are unhealthy.

History of hurts: a heart's emotional memory.

Meditative exercise: a short, creative narrative, imbued with visual imagery, meant to be read aloud in order to open the heart to God and His Word.

Rewind and reset: revisiting past relational conflict in order to evaluate healthy vs. unhealthy patterns.

WHOLE: An emotional power tool to implement when confronted by the hurtful words and actions of others. With repetitive practice and study, these five steps become second nature:

W = Welcome God in.
H = Hold fast to your truth.
O = Overcome Unhealthy Reactions
L = Listen between the Lines
E = Elevate the Atmosphere

How Do I Overcome Hurtful Words?

The LORD is close to the brokenhearted;
he rescues those whose spirits are crushed.
—Psalm 34:18 NLT

Hurtful words.

We've all heard them. Inside our homes, at work, on the playground, or at the sidelines of a sporting event. Sometimes they are delivered remotely via email, text, or social media, but they strike just as deep. These painful, disorienting words sting even more when delivered by people we thought we could trust. In the wake of such hurt, we stand frozen. Then, before we can take our next breath, our defense mechanisms kick into high gear and the fight, flight, or freeze zone in our brain sounds like a five-alarm fire. You know the feeling—heart racing, palms sweating, sick feeling in the pit of your stomach, flushing cheeks, and sometimes, an instant, pounding headache. It's all part of a purely natural instinct.

As a professional life coach, listening to the hearts of women is my *why*—why I do what I do. Day after day, they sit in my office, hearts battered and bruised by mean, hurtful words. Some women cry. Some are angry. Some are numb. Some want to disappear. All have one plea, "Help me," and one question, "How do I overcome these hurtful words?"

It's taken years of study and prayer and hundreds of conversations to even begin to answer this deeply challenging question. This is heart-wrenching, painful stuff we are talking about. And unfortunately, it's very real.

I don't know who or what has crushed your heart or how, but you are in the right place. Your weary heart has led you here. Someone's words have hurt you deeply, and you need help. You're desperate for answers. You've done your best to fix the situation yourself, but the hurt is too deep to heal on its own. It needs a second pair of eyes and ears to help process the pain. If your broken heart could talk, I think it might say, "Thank you for finally taking some time out to care for me. This is going to be so good."

Maybe you're standing in the aisle of your favorite bookstore, sitting with your computer in your dorm room, or searching Google for some much-needed advice—and you've found my book. This book is my humble and passionate effort to change the narrative of negative behavior. We need one another's stories—we all benefit when we write stories that bring light and love into the world. In a world at odds with itself, it is time to set aside the petty distractions that disconnect, and embrace the powerful cords that connect. I am convinced of one important truth: life is too short to waste entangled in or crushing others with our words. And when we do get entangled, it's because we are imperfect human beings. To maintain a vital relationship with God, self, and others, it is critical to untie the knots with wisdom, grace, and a deep, healthy respect for one another.

More than anything, I want to help you.

Yes, *you*. I want you to know that you are not alone. You do not have to write your story alone. As much as I would like to take away the pain of the hurtful words spoken to you, I can't. What I can do, however, is help you transform the pain inside your heart into something unimaginably powerful—an expansion of your heart's capacity and potential to live out its God-breathed purpose. I can't promise easy, but I can promise empowering. The God we serve is a turn-it-around God. Your pain will not be wasted. Genesis 50:20 assures this, "You intended to harm me, but God intended it for good to accomplish what is now being done, the saving of many lives." That's the remarkable way our God works.

Today is no ordinary day. It is the day you experience the power of a heartlift. I promise that your heart is going to feel so much better. Are you ready? Let's do this . . . together!

Always learning,

Janell

PART ONE: REFLECT

Present Pain:
Why Is This Happening?

Guard Your Heart

The Intention of Practice 1:
I will overcome hurtful words
by guarding my heart.

You've kept track of my every toss and turn
through the sleepless nights, each tear entered in your ledger,
each ache written in your book.
—Psalm 56:8 msg

Broken hearts do not discriminate. They beat inside the young, the old, the rich, the poor. They are color-blind, impartial, have no geographic boundaries, and are very personal. Say the word *broken-hearted*, and thoughts typically turn to a failed romance, yet heart-break often casts a wider net. When heartbreak happens because of hurtful words spoken by those we thought we could trust and those we hold closest to us, our hearts are crushed.

I thought they loved me.
I thought they had my back.
I thought I could trust them.

This crushing leaves *heartrifts*—deep, invisible wounds caused by hurtful words from close, trusted friends and family members. Left alone, heartrifts harbor within hearts for years, often lifetimes, and ultimately flow into families, communities, and churches—causing ever greater relationship rifts. Marriages fail. Families divide. Churches split. Governments implode.

A long time ago, the wise King Solomon said something very important about the heart. He wrote, "Above all else, guard your affections. For they influence everything else in your life" (Proverbs 4:23 TLB).

Above all else. No mincing of words here. These three little words indicate high priority status. Yet, we rarely take time out of our busy schedules to take care of our hearts. We might eat less red meat, exercise more, and drink plenty of water, but that isn't what King Solomon meant. He was talking about our emotional health and well-being—something we might rather push aside, sweep under the rug, or deal with later when we aren't so busy.

Experience the Power of a Heartlift

When given the time, energy, and attention they deserve, heartrifts slowly surrender to the power of a heartlift.

"Heartlift? What exactly is a heartlift, anyway?" you might ask.

You can look up *heartlift* in the dictionary, but you won't find a definition. It's an original thought, born through a great deal of prayer and life experience. Since founding my private coaching practice, I've walked alongside many women on their healing journeys. With great intention, I listen between the lines of my client's lives to hear the heartbeat of their stories. We talk about the current pain in their hearts. We look at their history of hurts. And together, we bring just enough of their past into the present so they can walk into the future with a whole and healed heart. I call this a heartlift.

Although I'd watched this approach lead to deep and meaningful breakthroughs for a long time, I'd struggled with what to call the process. Then, one spring afternoon while I was sitting in a hospital waiting room, a *TIME* magazine caught my eye. "Nip. Tuck. Or Else," read the cover story. One sentence in particular caught my attention: "In 2015 alone, women spent almost one billion dollars on facelifts."[1]

Did I read that right? I read it again, and yes, I'd read correctly.

The statistic stunned me. Kept circling in my head. Then I read on. Writer Joel Stein noted, "You're going to have to do it. And not all that long from now. Probably not a full-on, general-anesthesia bone shaving or muscle slicing. But almost definitely some injections into your face. . . . Not because you hate yourself, fear aging, or are vain. . . . You're going to get a cosmetic procedure for the same reason you wear makeup: because every other woman is."[2]

Because every other woman is? Am I reading this correctly?

Mr. Stein, I'm not one to debate, but I'd have to challenge your statements: "You are going to have to do it . . . definitely some injections in your face."

In my practice, listening to women's hearts is my *why*, and watching and reading faces is my *how*. Our faces mirror our hearts. Nonverbal cues and microexpressions say it all. Science of People founder Vanessa Van Edwards agrees that "learning how to decode the face is like having a super power."[3] *I want that super power.* Furrowed brows. Biting or pursing of the lips. Sad eyes. A twitch of the cheek. Chin pointed down. These microexpressions are "brief, involuntary facial expressions shown on the face of humans according to the emotions that are being experienced. Unlike regular, prolonged facial expressions, it is difficult to fake a microexpression."[4]

I was explaining this to a client one day. "You're like a face whisperer," she said. "I can't hide anything from you."

"I'm a heartlifter," I reminded her. "The words we speak come straight out of our hearts. Luke 6:45 says, 'A good man brings good things out of the good stored up in his heart, and an evil man brings evil things out of the evil stored up in his heart. For the mouth speaks what the heart is full of.' The way I see it, we're all just big walking hearts bumping into each other, aren't we? So I pay close attention, that's all. Hearts matter to me.

"Most importantly," I continued, "*your* heart matters to me. Describe how you feel when your heart lets go of something painful. Do you experience anything physical?"

"Definitely. It feels like . . . psychological brightness." She smiled.

"That is a fabulous description. I've never heard that anywhere. I think you are on to a brand-new psychological term. Let's keep that psychological brightness on that beautiful face of yours!"

Facial expressions say way more than words. As my client discovered, when her heart experiences the release of painful, often embedded, memories or emotions, she experiences an actual "brightening." Not only is her face brighter, her entire being is lighter. Proverbs 15:13 affirms this finding: "A happy heart makes the face cheerful, but heartache crushes the spirit."

Experts agree: "When we make facial expressions, we're essentially transmitting a packet of information that can be received, read, and interpreted by others. By contracting or expanding our facial muscles in different degrees and combinations, we can produce thousands of different messages that provide cues to our overall emotional state, our short-term feelings about our immediate environment, our mental well-being, our personality and mood, our physical health, our credibility, and whether or not we view others as being creditable."[5]

The bottom line is that absolutely everything in our lives comes back to the condition of our hearts.

Through the years, the pain women express has less to do with outer appearance and much to do with the deep pain and percolating discontent inside their hearts. Once the pain lifts, the entire countenance changes. They look and feel so much better. Psychological brightness!

And then I realized—what women most need is a heartlift, a facelift on the inside. When a woman's heart is welcomed into a safe place with a trusted person, it moves through the process of vocalizing crushing pain in a healthy manner that brings closure, emotional healing, and lasting freedom.

Right then and there, I knew I wanted to spend the rest of my life offering women the power of a heartlift. Real, lasting change—from the inside out.

The Unexpected Emotional Earthquake

If you are holding this book in your hands, you are holding a heart crushed by feuds in family lineage, surprised by the hurtful words and actions of others, disoriented by dysfunctional relationships, and shaken by a loss of faith in people I trusted. These slow-forming fissures began when I was very young, way before I even knew or understood heartbreak existed, until one day it was unmistakable. Heartrifts in deep need of healing had formed along the contours of my heart. Time takes a toll on the heart and, after a while, mine simply couldn't take any more. *Boom*—it broke into a million little pieces. And if you're reading this book, you've probably experienced this too.

As a longtime resident of the East Coast, I am all too accustomed to nasty nor'easters, hair-raising hurricanes, and even the occasional tornado, but never in a million years would the residents of my state expect an earthquake in Virginia. Imagine my surprise, then, on an ordinary hot and humid August afternoon when all of a sudden, I heard and felt a very loud, very scary *boom*! The earth and everything beneath me started shaking. My hands gripped the chair I was sitting in. For a few seconds—though it felt like hours—my heart stopped.

What was that?

At first, I didn't know what was going on. Nothing fell off the walls, even though things were a bit crooked and disheveled. A little off-center myself, I closed the book I'd been reading and looked through the shades. Everything seemed normal. The sky was bright blue, and the sun was still shining.

Thoughts raced through my head. *Should I run for cover? Did a bomb go off? Did something crash outside?* We lived in an area with thriving shipyards and fortified naval bases, so this was a very real possibility.

Suddenly, the phone rang. My husband. "Did you feel that?" The panic in his voice matched the panic I felt inside. "Turn on the TV."

I wrestled with the morning paper on the couch, trying to find the remote. *Is this really happening?* I wondered.

"Oh! Rob, we had an earthquake," I said. "The newscasters are as stunned as we are. This is unbelievable. Are you okay?"

"Yeah, shaken up, that's all. How about you?"

We listened to the news together, recovering a sense of balance and strength from one another. Sure enough, the broadcasters confirmed that we'd had a 5.8 magnitude earthquake, right here in Virginia. The epicenter was about 150 miles northwest of our home. For months after this ordeal, community officials revisited the situation, offering ways to prepare in case it happens again. In fact, this seismic shaking is still talked about today.

Three Phases of a Heartlift

Our hearts, like the fault lines of the Virginia seismic zone, can reach a breaking point. Life suddenly becomes too much to bear. Unexpected, startling words or actions cause an emotional upheaval evidenced by shock, anger, despair, or worse, retaliation. When this happens, we must be prepared. The whirlwind of our whys cries out for immediate answers. *Why is this happening to me? Why can't I get it right? Why is God doing this to me?* Processing the whys becomes increasingly important to our healing journey.

My prayer for your heartlift journey is threefold: (1) that your current heartrift experiences will heal; (2) that you will be empowered and equipped, through the nine practices I outline in this book, to experience your very own heartlift; and (3) that your heartlift toolbox gains practical, effective, and spiritually mature tools to help both you and everyone in your sphere of influence to live their remarkable, God-created lives.

Overcoming Hurtful Words is divided into three sections, based on the three phases of the heartlift journey:

1. Reflect: *Heartrift—what just happened?*
   Welcome God into the whys of present pain.
2. Reframe: *Heartsift—where did it come from?*
   Face the fault lines of past hurts.

3. Reauthor: *Heartlift—will I trust again?*
   Live in newfound freedom in Christ.

Practice Makes Progress

Each section of this book contains three chapters that serve as guides along the way. They're born from my conversations with women who've experienced their own heartlifts. Instead of calling them chapters, we will call them practices, because *Overcoming Hurtful Words* invites us to begin practicing self-care and to exercise new behavior patterns and communication skills. I wish I could wave my nice-and-easy wand, but I'm afraid that isn't the reality of change. Change takes a great deal of practice.

For most of my life, I equated *practice* with *perfection*. I came by this mind-set honestly. As a six-year-old, I began baton twirling lessons. Before we could leave our weekly class session, the teacher insisted we complete a double turn. If I did two spins, I did a thousand. Over and over again, my little six-year-old frame stood ready and willing. *You've got this.* Throw, turn, drop. Repeat. *Ugh!* Every time I tried, that slippery silver stick fell to the ground. I couldn't figure out how to throw the baton in the air, spin on one foot, and catch the thing when I'd finished turning. But my teacher, Susan Cappeletto, Miss Majorette of America, assured me if I practiced harder, it would happen.

All these years later, however, my thoughts have changed. Life isn't about practicing harder or practicing until it's perfect; it's about practicing and making progress. All those hours of practicing double turns and twirling techniques did teach me this though: there is great value in the discipline of practice.

The world we live in feeds a perfectionist mind-set with its persistent, demanding messages of *more, more, more* and *better, better,*

better. So, while we're on this heartlift journey, it will be important that we keep one truth in the forefront of our minds: practice isn't about perfection. It's all about progress—moving forward on a glorious journey of discovering and becoming the remarkable women God created us to be.

When we activate the nine practices presented in this book on a daily basis, they will become second nature. The old, unhealthy ways will slowly, certainly, and a bit magically transform into a new, healthy way of life (see 2 Corinthians 5:17). We practice everything else in the world—why not practice healthy behavior patterns and healthy communication skills? They are at the core of life. When we operate from a healthy foundation, the world is a better place.

At the end of each practice is a section called Heart Care, which will include exercises for the three phases of the heartlift. These exercises will help you move through your heartbreak to the wholeness you so desire.

- ***Reflect:*** includes meditations taken from the wisdom of the book of Proverbs, teachings from Jesus, the Gospels, and letters written by Paul, particularly his letters to the Ephesians and Philippians. These sacred writings are filled with passionate teaching and wisdom about the inner workings of the heart and the complexities of human relationships. In this section, we'll use a traditional Benedictine practice called *lectio divina* (divine reading). This is a contemplative approach to reading Scripture that teaches us to read the passage slowly, savoring it word by word and placing ourselves within its context. We'll ask, "What here speaks to me? Is there a word, a thought, or perhaps a visual that I want to more deeply consider?" This exercise appeals to the senses and invites us to lean in and listen for the whispers of God. While lectio divina is traditionally done in a group of four to eight people, it is certainly applicable to individual meditation, as well.

- *Reframe:* entails relevant, practical exercises for reframing unhealthy thoughts and patterns into healthy ones. This includes meditative exercises, Scripture reading, charts, and illustrations. This is time for practical application in your daily life; for making changes, implementing new skills, and establishing healthy principles.

- *Reauthor:* involves creative journaling techniques and positive prompts for reauthoring the nine practices into a new narrative. During my master's course of study, professors presented and discussed many therapeutic and counseling methodologies. One in particular—narrative therapy—appealed to me because of my love for writing, personal narrative, and inner healing. Developed by Australian social workers Michael White and David Epston, narrative therapy believes that

As humans, we are interpreting beings. We all have daily experiences of events that we seek to make meaningful. The stories we have about our lives are created through linking certain events together in a particular sequence across a time period, and finding a way of explaining or making sense of them. A narrative is like a thread that weaves the events together, forming a story.[6]

As you move through the threads that weave your heartrift narrative, you will reauthor it. You will write a new narrative by which you will live out your newfound freedom in Christ.

Finally, I must warn you. I am crazy about words and their meanings, so understanding the heart of a word is a big deal. As you read, pretend we are in a face-to-face coaching session, where we would peel a word like an apple until we get to the core. There, we'll find the seeds, the words within the word. Knowing the literal translation of a word provides inside information that can become a useful and empowering tool for reauthoring our stories.

The Great Heartlift Challenge

Our hearts won't heal if we don't offer them healing. We have a big part to play in making change happen. As a dear client of mine, Gina, says, "Nothing changes if nothing changes. It stays the same, which is really sad. Or, the saddest of all, it gets worse and robs us of living a meaningful life." She is so right.

I pray my story informs your story and helps ease your hurting heart. I am here to "call back" to you, as L. B. Cowman so eloquently expresses in this poem, "Call Back":

If you have gone a little way ahead of me, call back—
'Twill cheer my heart and help my feet along the stony track;
And if, perchance, Faith's light is dim, because the oil is low,
Your call will guide my lagging course as wearily I go.

Call back, and tell me that He went with you into the storm;
Call back, and say He kept you when the forest's roots
 were torn;
That, when the heavens thunder and the earthquake shook
 the hill,
He bore you up and held you where the very air was still.

Oh, friend, call back, and tell me, for I cannot see your face,
They say it glows with triumph, and your feet bound in
    the race;
But there are mists between us and my spirit eyes are dim,
And I cannot see the glory, though I long for word of Him.

But if you'll say He heard you when your prayer was but a cry,
And if you'll say He saw you through the night's sin-darkened
    sky
If you have gone a little way ahead, oh, friend, call back—
'Twill cheer my heart and help my feet along the stony track.[7]

I am calling back to you. Every word of this poem is true. God
has brought me through, and He will do the same for you. Together,
we'll welcome Him into this heartlifting safe space, grounded in
trust and authentic love, and let the heart care happen. Together,
we'll work through the pages of your story and spend time reauthoring your narrative. Mingled throughout the practices are meditative
exercises—short, creative stories that invite us to "be still, and
know that I am God" (Psalm 46:10). Ever the teacher, I will review,
review, and review some more. Indulge me; there is a method to
my madness.

You Will Find Your Smile Again

Don't worry, when it gets tough, I'll pick you up. When you fall, I'll
do my best to soften the ground. When you are tired, I'll cheer you
on. I'm not leaving your side until the scary place of pain transforms
into the sacred space of security and peace. We can turn to wise King
Solomon, who said it best:

Two can accomplish more than twice as much as one, for the results can be much better. If one falls, the other pulls him up; but if a man falls when he is alone, he's in trouble. . . . And one standing alone can be attacked and defeated, but two can stand back-to-back and conquer; three is even better, for a triple-braided cord is not easily broken
—Ecclesiastes 4:9–12 TLB

That's the deal: you, me, and God—a powerful, triple-braided cord. I am confident of one thing: you will find your smile again. I found mine, and I'm here to help you find yours. Before we begin this transformative journey, may I pray this prayer of blessing over you? I like to think of it as our heartlifter's prayer.

Dear God,

No one knows pain like You. Please come alongside my new friend. Walk every single step of this hard-but-worth-it journey with her. Surround her with Your healing wings (Psalm 91). As she reviews the tender, broken places in her heart, I pray You will visit her with the miraculous healing that comes only from You.

Where there is despair, bring the bright dawn of a brand-new beginning. Where there are lies, bring the light of truth. Where there is hate, bring a love that comes only from You. Where there is unforgiveness, bring the supernatural capacity to let go. Where there is anger, bring the peace that passes all understanding. Where there is confusion, bring clarity and vision. Where there is oppression, bring the freedom of the cross. Where there is sadness, bring joy unspeakable and full of glory.

Help her rise above her crushing heartrift and bring her to rejoice in her powerful heartlift. Most of all, help her remember that she needs to take really good care of her heart. Teach her to guard her affections, for they influence everything in her life.

Amen.

HEART CARE

When beginning any journey, either physical or spiritual, preparation is key. This journey will require time, space, and, as we say in the South, sheer guts and grit. It might not be easy, but the end result will be a brand-new healthy heart, pounding with a capacity to love again. *Ah, what a great thought.*

First things first—be sure to join our online community, Overcoming Hurtful Words, at www.overcominghurtfulwords.com. We are so much better together. Then, find a quiet place where you can study. Set a beautiful table (just for fun) and brew a pot of your favorite tea or coffee. My favorite is Kericho Gold Premium Tea, found while traveling in Kenya. Maybe we can share a cup one day. What's yours?

Okay, are you ready to begin? Let's do this! Grab your journal and a pen. It might help to write down what you learn. Now, take a deep breath. This Heart Care requires a little bit of time, a whole lot of energy, and a big dose of courage.

Reflect

Here, at the onset of your heartlift practice, take some time to read several passages from Ephesians 4 (AMP), written by the apostle Paul. Even though they were written so many years ago, the words remain applicable, relevant, and they help us see the importance of mature behavior(s). He uses phrases like I appeal to you . . . Make every effort . . . Let us grow up . . . because Paul's heart wanted every single person in his sphere of influence, and beyond, to be mature. As you read, consider—maybe even highlight—what characteristics define a "mature person." Is this something "easy" to obtain or perhaps a process of day-to-day intentions and practices?

Ephesians 4:1–3, "So, I, the prisoner for the Lord, appeal to you to live a life worthy of the calling to which you have been called [that is, to live a life that exhibits godly character, moral courage, personal integrity, and mature behavior—a life that expresses gratitude to God for your salvation], with all humility [forsaking self-righteousness], and gentleness [maintaining self-control], with patience, bearing with one another in [unselfish] love. Make every effort to keep the oneness of the Spirit in the bond of peace [each individual working together to make the whole successful.]"

Ephesians 4:13–16, "Until we all reach oneness in the faith and in the knowledge of the Son of God, [growing spiritually] to become a mature believer, reaching to the measure of the fullness of Christ [manifesting His spiritual completeness and exercising our spiritual gifts in unity]. So that we are no longer children [spiritually immature], tossed back and forth [like ships on a stormy sea] and carried about by every wind of [shifting] doctrine, by the cunning and trickery of [unscrupulous] men, by the deceitful scheming of people ready to do anything [for personal profit]. But speaking the truth in love [in all things—both our speech and our lives expressing His truth], let us grow up in all things into Him [following His example] who is the Head—Christ. From Him the whole body [the church, in all its various parts], joined and knitted firmly together by what every joint supplies, when each part is working properly, causes the body to grow and mature, building itself up in [unselfish] love."

Reframe

In your journal, write a note to yourself (or to God—that's what I like to do) and share your realistic expectations or desires for what you would like to see God do in your heart, in a specific relationship, or in all your relationships as a whole. Begin an honest, healing conversation with yourself about your heart's history of hurts. We all have one.

Take the Heartlift Checkup.

Ask yourself,

- Is my heart hurting so badly I can hardly stand it?
- Is it tender to the touch and guarded?
- Is it confused, bewildered, or stunned?
- Is it angry, tense, or terrified?
- Is it numb or, even worse, so tired it wants to call it quits?
- Is it closed completely with a Do Not Disturb sign hanging on its door?
- Or am I halfway to healing and just need a little help to finish?

Reauthor

Borrowing from the geological world, a fault line is a break in the earth's crust where various stressors cause the constant shifting of tectonic plates. This causes slippage and, eventually, an earthquake. Our hearts have fault lines too, and we need to examine them. We will identify these deep stresses as *heartrifts*, fault lines that may eventually reach their breaking point. *Our hearts can't take any more.*

Simple questions to ask yourself in evaluation might be:

- How am I doing physically and emotionally (the visible realm)?
- How am I doing psychologically and spiritually (the invisible realm)?
- Which of these stressors affects my fault lines:
  - People pleasing?
  - Approval seeking?
  - Overachieving?
  - Legalism?
  - Shaming?
  - Perfectionism?
  - Fear of rejection?
  - Excessive worry?
  - Repressed or suppressed anger?
  - Insecurity or inferiority?
  - Caring too much?
  - Not knowing how or when to say no?
  - _____? (Fill in the blank)

These questions can feel overwhelming, but you are not alone. You can find community online at www.overcominghurtfulwords. com. Better than that, God has promised to stay by your side. It's time to move forward to healing. In this moment of decision, make the pledge.

The *Overcoming Hurtful Words* Pledge

Today, I pledge that I am ready, willing, and able to commit to this heartlift journey. I know it will require honesty, hard work, and a big dose of humility. When the going gets tough, I will remember that God, the author and finisher of my faith (Hebrews 12:1–2) is with me, even if, at times, I feel as though I am all alone. His silence is not His neglect; He knows the perfect time, has the perfect plan, and is never late (Ecclesiastes 3:14). He will help me move through this scary place of pain and into the beautiful, sacred space of peace, so that I can live, love, and laugh again. When I need help, I will ask for it. When I want to isolate myself and hide away, I will instead seek the company of wise women who will walk beside me. When I need courage, I will whisper my brave, three-word prayer—*God help me.* Amen.

Signed, this _____ day of _____ (month/year),

_____

PRACTICE 2

Welcome God into the Whys

The Intention of Practice 2:
I will overcome hurtful words
by welcoming God into my whys.

I don't hold to the idea that God causes suffering and crisis.
I just know that those things come along and God uses them.
We think life should be a nice, clean ascending line.
But inevitably something wanders onto the scene and creates
havoc with the nice way we've arranged life to fall in place.[8]
—Sue Monk Kidd

Without a doubt, the perplexing pain of a crushed heart craves isolation. It longs to sit alone in a room, lights out, covers over the head. But we must be careful. Danger lurks in the darkness of such a scary space. When we close the blinds of our world in this manner, we open ourselves to an even greater sadness that can lead into the rubble of depression, self-loathing, and the perilous pit of self-pity.

Without a doubt—and please hear my heart here—we must welcome God into the aching abyss of our pain. He can handle it, and He will help you handle it.

You may manage only a windless whisper-prayer like *God help me*, but there is more power in those words than you can ever imagine. Take a moment, right now. Close your eyes. Open your hands— palms up—ready to receive your blessing from a God who sees and loves you very much. It might not *feel* as if He sees, but please trust me—as a woman who has been where you are, I know. He sees you. He tells us He will never, ever leave us or forsake us (Deuteronomy 31:6), and He doesn't.

> *God, please be with me.*
> *This pain is too much to bear.*
> *God, please be with me.*

How can I be so sure? Because one Saturday afternoon, He heard my whisper-prayer and helped me out of a very dark place.

A Saturday Afternoon
God Help Me Prayer

Living near the Atlantic coast means living with many bridges and tunnels. Where there is water, there must be ways to cross it. That means travel here usually requires timing both expected and unexpected bridge and tunnel traffic. On my way home from a meeting where a serious altercation had arisen between me and a fellow leader, I crossed one of our region's longer bridge-tunnels.

I sat there in my car, and my mind kept hitting the rewind button, replaying every ugly scene as if it were a movie. Only this was real life—my life. Despair sat shotgun, and Negative Thoughts camped in the backseat, taunting my mind like hungry, tired, twin toddlers. They gave it all they had.

Angela and I had disagreed about something *again*. It was yet another agitating confrontation that had sent my mind reeling. It was a low point, for sure. Something about her commanding presence intimidated me and within seconds, *boom*! tears had flowed and my heart was in panic mode. I'd had one thought—*why is this happening?* Her stoic, stern presence was so reminiscent of the Catholic nuns of my childhood. The shame-filled, hurtful words she'd spoken over me had effectively shut me down. I'd wanted to respond but felt emotionally paralyzed, unable to even speak. My soul literally trembled as I felt a sudden shift in the fault lines of my heart. At that moment, a heartrift was born.

Midway through the bridge crossing, more negative thoughts washed over my mind. One seemed to yell the loudest: *Just drive off the bridge. Would anyone really care?*

I make no excuses. I can't hide the fact that I was deeply wounded by key people in my church—leaders who, I thought, controlled whether I had a voice in our church—and Angela was one of them. After years of subtle, oppressive, unhealthy attempts at silencing my voice and ministry, the pain had taken its toll. My deepest desire was to be in a community where my God-given gifts and talents could help others. I didn't necessarily need a fairy-tale ending where everyone rallies around the campfire, makes s'mores, and sings "Kumbaya," but I desperately wanted my church relationships, including the one with Angela, to work.

More than anything, I wanted people to treat each other better. The fact that we weren't getting along broke my heart. I sincerely believe a church is supposed to be the safest of all safe places. Not perfect, but a haven in which our hearts can rest. But it seemed God had something else in mind. All I knew was that, for the first time in a long time, I found myself unable to put on that well-trained, perfectly shaped, everything-is-fine-really-it-is smile. A lifetime of pretense—living with the pain and shame of an alcoholic father and then living a life of on-stage performance via dance, theater, and competitive beauty pageants—had taught me that smile. I owned it.

It's amazing how good we become at hiding behind our smiles.

In times of conflict like the meeting that day, we often ask, "Why can't we get along? Why is this relationship so terribly difficult? What am I doing wrong here?" For some reason that I didn't understand at the time, nothing I tried (note: *I tried*)—praying harder, working harder, believing harder—made staying in this particular relationship work. The heartrift remained. After years of futile attempts and exhausting efforts to become who and what she and the powers to be at our church wanted me to be, it was time for a change. Ultimately, the painful confrontation with Angela made the push to leave the relationship stronger than the pull to stay.

Welcome God into the Whys

With tears streaming down my face, I finally made it to the other side of the bridge. That two-minute crossing felt like an eternity. Miles later, as I rounded the corner of the exit leading home, I found a spot to park the car for a few minutes. Overwhelmed by it all, I needed to pull myself together. I also needed to welcome God into the devastating whirlwind of whys that were tossing me to-and-fro like a ship in a storm. Somehow, I kept my head above water and managed a prayer. It went something like this:

God, what on earth is happening here? Why is this relationship hitting me so hard? Part of me just wants to die. Please help me understand the whys of this circumstance—or better yet, the how to keep moving forward. Why, oh why, is this woman, who calls herself my friend, treating me so harshly? The worst part is how it's all hidden behind that façade of a well-groomed smile. I know there is something for me to learn through all this.

And then, I whispered those welcoming words: *God, please help me.*

I wanted to give up, but in that moment, something special happened. It seemed like God took a big sifter into His hands and shook the truth from the lies. The stubborn clumps of negative emotions and self-defeating confusion were revealed, aerated by His breath of truth.

I literally felt a release. Something lifted. I felt lighter. A definite, emotional shift had happened deep in my core. The trembling stopped, peace settled in, and my breathing became easier. There was no audible voice; no angelic choir sang—yet something was different.

Subtly, powerfully, I heard God whisper back to me, "*Don't listen to those lies. Her words are from the father of lies (John 8:44) who wants to destroy you. Breathe. Remember whose you are. Listen to Me.*"

As I welcomed God into my whys, a clear choice came to mind. I could listen to the lies of the negative committee inside my head, call it quits, and drive off the bridge of life. *Or . . .* I could listen to the truth. I could build a bridge of hope and healing for myself and help other women do the same.

There was no in-between. I had a decision to make.

When We Need to Change

On that fateful day when I pulled my car over to pray, I spoke some painful words—"part of me just wants to die." I did not know the power inside those words. In hindsight, I see that part of me *needed* to die. Not literally, of course, but my unhealthy, people-pleasing, approval-addicted, applause-hungry self needed to die before my healthy, God-created identity and capacity would flourish.

What happened next surprised me.

Welcoming God into our whys changes everything. It creates an entirely different perspective and framework for our emotions. This emotional shift, which I now call a *heartshift*, defines the specific moment on a life map where we awaken to truth. Truth about God. Truth about ourselves. Truth about others.

The entire situation had nothing to do with Angela and everything to do with me. The heartshift came when I realized it wasn't Angela who needed to change. *I needed to change.* I needed to accept my God-created value, worth, and dignity; to live worthy of my calling (Ephesians 4:1). I needed to accept my responsibility in the unhealthy nature of our relationship. What role did I play in all this? Relationships are rarely one-sided.

At the end of the day, I couldn't change or fix Angela, but I could help myself change. Of course, my acknowledging this did not in any way let Angela off the hook for her behavior—but realizing she was responsible for herself released me to focus my energy on what was most important: I am responsible only for my own actions, behaviors, and words. I must commit to becoming healthy and whole—and that commitment is not dependent on anyone but myself. But first, I had to let go of the hurts Angela had caused me, so that I could move on.

Isn't that what forgiveness is all about? Renowned Christian author Lewis Smedes reminds us,

> To forgive is to set a prisoner free and discover that the prisoner was you. Forgiving does not erase the bitter past. A healed memory is not a deleted memory. Instead, forgiving what we cannot forget creates a new way to remember. We change the memory of our past into a hope for our future. You will know that forgiveness has begun when you recall those who hurt you and feel the power to wish them well.[9]

As hard as this truth was to swallow, I had to admit I'd allowed Angela, and many people before her, to take control in my life. For the first time, I realized this behavior had to stop.

Once again, I prayed. This time, I asked God to forgive me. Yes, *me*. I had allowed people to be bigger and more powerful in my life than God. I had given them permission to make decisions for me. To tell me what I should and shouldn't be. Somewhere in the story of my life, I had given my pen to others and, in return, had lost my authentic voice, my God-given vision, and sadly, my promised victory. The psalmist David reminds us that in doing this, we are allowing human opinion to disable us (Proverbs 29:25 MSG). To keep us from living a God-created, meaningful life (John 10:10). Not one free from pain or suffering—that is impossible. But one in which we live from an authentic place.

So right there on the side of an ordinary road, my heartlift journey started. At my darkest hour, God reached down from heaven and offered His hand to me. That's the beauty about God. Logistics don't seem to matter; God meets us right where we are. *In the privacy of*

our home. On the side of the road. In the middle of a crowded classroom.
When we finally surrender our need to know the whys, to get revenge or retaliation, or even to have the last word, the heartrift releases us—its strong grip weakened by our sincere desire to be freed from its oppressive clasp.

I like to think God gave me my pen back. Invited me to begin reauthoring my story—one in which I collaborate with God, the author and finisher of my faith (Hebrews 12:1–2)—and move through life from a healthy place with a healthy sense of self, healthy behavior patterns, and healthy communication skills.

Today, God is giving you your pen back, too. He's inviting you to experience the power of a heartlift. Unsure of how to begin? Let's start together.

Five Steps toward Being WHOLE

Because I am a visual learner and needed a lot of help to process someone's hurtful words, I created a simple, five-step power tool I call *WHOLE*. I have a sense it might help you too. Think of yourself as a "hurtful words first responder"—the one who shows up first in a relational crisis. When an emotional earthquake hits or you collide with someone else's raging fault lines, activate WHOLE. The more you use this tool, the more it will become second nature. The goal is to respond, not react.

Rehearsing these steps establishes the framework for transforming heartrifting words into healthy, heartlifting conversations. The five steps include:

W: Welcome God in
H: Hold fast to your truth

O: Overcome unhealthy reactions

L: Listen between the lines

E: Elevate the atmosphere

W: Welcome God in

When we're confronted with someone's unhealthy behavior, anger, shock, and confusion can set in. Without a doubt, our initial reaction is to ask why this is happening to us. Instead of letting these emotions take control, practice taking a step back (either literally or mentally), welcome God in, and whisper a brave three-word prayer—*God help me*. And then, breathe.

Yes, breathe. Let me explain. In this sense, *breathe* means "to pause to rest or regain breath and composure."[10] Composure is that innate "state or sense of being calm and in control of oneself."[11] This takes practicing something called *emotional regulation*, or the ability to manage and maintain our emotional state under any circumstance. Highly complex, but God is able to help and empower this capacity. Biblical language calls this self-control (Galatians 5:22–23). When the affront happens, it feels very personal—and it sincerely is personal. Yet by stepping back and intentionally applying emotional regulation, we can depersonalize it and allow the necessary space to gain the much-needed composure we talked about earlier.

"Between stimulus and response, there is a space," writes psychiatrist Viktor Frankl. "In that space is our power to choose our response. In our response lies our growth and our freedom."[12] (We'll talk more about this in the "E" of our WHOLE power tool.)

After the shock wears off, two important things must happen. They seem to be contrary to each another, so there will be tension here.

First, we must ***assess the situation.*** Ask yourself, Do I treat this comment like a duck would? Let it roll off my back like water? Proverbs 19:11 supports this response: "A person's wisdom yields patience; it is to one's glory to overlook an offense." We all say stupid, nonsensical, off-the-cuff comments at times that could potentially hurt someone's feelings. Words hold this power. They bring life or death (Proverbs 18:21). No in-between here, either. Contrary to the childhood rhyme about sticks and stones breaking bones but words never hurting, words do hurt; I'm very sure we all agree here. In truth, words can break hearts.

Second, we must ***address the situation.*** Decide whether to address the hurtful statement with immediate candor or at a later date, one-on-one, with a witness or mediator present, especially if the confrontation is volatile or heated. (See Matthew 18:15–20.)

I call this process "Rewind and Reset." Sometimes we need to give the situation or circumstance some space and time. We need time to breathe. Maybe we seek wise counsel so as to thoroughly assess the situation. When we rewind and reset, we ask the all-important questions: *How could I have handled this better? What is my responsibility? What is the next healthy step?*

Women speak an average of twenty thousand words a day—of course we are bound to mess up. A wise woman once shared with me how she starts her day. Before her feet ever hit the ground, she prays the words of Psalm 19:14, "May these words of my mouth and this meditation of my heart be pleasing in your sight, LORD, my Rock and my Redeemer." I think that is good advice.

As I rewound and reset the situation with Angela, I realized the entire situation could have been avoided if I had been operating from a healthy sense of self, which we will talk about more in Practice 3. But at that time in my life, I wasn't. Sadly, I needed her approval, and I gave her more power in my life than I gave God.

Proverbs 29:25 helps clarify the dangers of people pleasing. Solomon warns, "The fear of human opinion disables; trusting in God protects you from that" (msg). Edward T. Welch, author of *When People Are Big and God Is Small*, writes, "Fear in the biblical sense . . . includes being afraid of someone, but it extends to holding someone in awe, being controlled or mastered by people, worshipping other people, putting your trust in people, or needing people."[13]

Angela was in charge of the women's ministry at my church, so basically my teaching ministry at this particular church was in her hands, but if I had been healthier, my trust would have been in God's divine direction over where and when and how and why I was to lead and teach, not in Angela's seeming control over my life.

This is true in any setting. My struggle happened within the context of ministry and church. Yours might be at work, on the sidelines of your child's athletic events, or right within your own family. Setting is important, but even more important is this truth: giving anyone this kind of power diminishes and devalues our sense of worth and dignity. We are to be respectful, yes, but our ultimate allegiance is to God, and our ultimate identity comes from God, not man. When we value ourselves, we value our voice. We don't let anyone devalue us.

H: Hold Fast to Your Truth

The definition of *hold fast* is: "to bear down, grit it out, stay the course. Originally a nautical term probably borrowed from the Dutch *houd vast* (hold tight) referring to the importance of securely gripping a ship's rigging."[14]

Remember that emotional regulation we talked about? When the initial hurtful words are hurled at us, we often retaliate or react. Sometimes, we do nothing at all. In light of this, it is critical that we hold fast to truth. Before we blink, we must hold fast to our truth. We tell ourselves we have God-breathed value, worth, and dignity. We hold fast to our tongues, our reactions, and our retaliation instinct, in order to practice our healthy responses. Our highest goal is to respond, not react. Is it easy? No. Possible? Yes.

Don't feed the fire of mean. The spirit of unhealthy behavior is like a fire—feed it, and it burns hotter. If you retaliate unhealthy with unhealthy, mean with mean, anger with anger, hate with hate, impatience with impatience, jealousy with jealousy, and so on, the battle will only get fiercer. Our enemy loves a good fight (Ephesians 6:12).

Instead, detach and decide. The spirit of unhealthy behavior needs water thrown on it. Detach yourself and decide to either stand firm against it or walk away until the situation cools down or a witness is available to accompany you to a meeting where an actual healing conversation can occur. Does yelling ever make a situation better? Does spewing harsh words ever solve anything? No. They make things worse. For example, *mean* is normally accompanied by *intimidation*—a deadly combination that makes the recipient feel like a speck of dust.

Imagine you are in the desert on a beautiful nature hike. Suddenly, a copperhead strikes, and its poison enters your body. This lethal bite will require immediate attention by trained doctors, most likely in an emergency room. An antidote must be administered. Oh, how I wish we had emergency rooms for the bites of people. Instead, we have an Almighty God, an even better place to run. At His feet, He administers the antidote of His love.

O: Overcome Unhealthy [Reactions] with Healthy [Responses]

Overcome is a powerful word. In fact, it's one we hear a great deal about but might not really understand. If and when we grasp its true power, watch out! One translation of the Greek word *yakol* means "able to gain or accomplish; able to endure; able to reach; to have ability or strength."[15] The key here is *being able*. Going one step further, *able* means "having the power, skill, means, or opportunity to do something." Can you see me doing my happy dance right now?

We are able to reframe unhealthy interpersonal relationship skills in order to practice healthy ones. We have the God-breathed capacity (see Practice 3) to do this.

From this moment forward, our heartlift journey is framed in two words: *healthy* and *unhealthy*. Without a doubt, this reframing will take God's help, but without intentional action, I'm not sure our heartrifts can truly heal. They will remain locked behind those prison bars of unforgiveness, bitterness, grudges, and division.

L: Lean in and Listen between the Lines

The real challenge here is remembering that the highest form of love is often tough love—love that sets limits and defines boundaries. Always remind yourself, "I have value, worth, and dignity. I will not be spoken to in this tone or manner. When I can talk with this person in a calmer, more collected way, we will talk." This will take loads of practice and some hard-earned patience, especially when someone is spewing hurtful words. You might need another deep breath of composure and a big heaping of emotional regulation. Ask this one question: Is this comment/action symptomatic of something deeper going on?

Dr. Elke Rechberger defines this as "listening between the lines" or "getting to what isn't being said."[16] This form of active listening is foundational to getting to the heart of the matter. "Listening is a magnetic and strange thing, a creative force," writes psychiatrist Karl Menninger, founder of the famed Menninger Clinic in Topeka,

Kansas. "The friends who listen to us are the ones we move toward, and we want to sit in their radius. When we are listened to, it creates us, makes us unfold and expand."[17]

Ruth and Janet were friends who could lean in and listen to each other. They knew they were safe in each other's radius. They went away one weekend for some much needed rest and relaxation. While getting dressed for dinner, Ruth became frustrated with her outfit selection.

"I shouldn't have waited until the last minute to pack," she said. "I just threw things into my suitcase, and nothing is working. I can't do anything right." Totally exasperated, she collapsed on the bed.

"Hey," Janet said, sitting next to her. "Wait a minute. We're talking clothes here. What's going on? You look great."

"Ugh. I am so dang inadequate," Ruth cried. "Inadequate."

At that moment, bells went off inside Janet's head. Somewhere between packing and a dinner outfit, Ruth had belittled herself and claimed she couldn't do anything right. As Janet leaned in and listened between the lines of Ruth's words, she knew they needed to talk this one through.

Having women in our lives who lean in and really listen is the beauty of authentic friendship. It provides the breathing room needed to process a situation. And that breathing room leads us right here, right now, as we learn from past mistakes so we can live in lasting freedom.

Ruth and Janet talked late into the night. Little by little, they unveiled some underlying faulty thinking that allowed Ruth to realize the roots of her feeling inadequate. Ruth felt confident that the heartlift would continue to give her insights and wisdom. They drove home brighter and lighter than they had felt on the way to their weekend away.

E: Elevate the Atmosphere

"I'm asking you to come up higher—a lot higher, I know." This is something I tell my clients often. When we've been hurt by someone's raging fault lines, the last thing we want to do is "elevate the atmosphere," but with God's help, it's what we must do. Why? The higher road is what moves us through the heartbreak and into the realm of personal maturity. And ultimately, it glorifies God, because we've responded in a way that helps, not hinders, His presence in the lives around us. This movement toward healthy creates that healthy atmosphere we're talking about. People want to be in the same space with us.

Consider the Latin root of elevate: *elevat*, meaning "raised,"[18] is derived from the verb *elevare*, e + levare (from *levis*, "light") = lighten. We know that feeding the fire of unhealthy behavior is only going to make the situation more difficult, so we must practice taking the higher road. Be the one in the room who is in that very important space Frankl spoke about; be the one who somehow equalizes and lightens the raging fault lines. In that space between stimulus and response, we choose the mature response. We choose to be the one filled with God's breath, not our own. Then we are filled with God's capacity to change the entire situation for the good of everyone involved.

This is not easy. It takes practice. It might require getting professional help. Getting help is a sign of strength, not weakness. It's a sign of wisdom, as Proverbs 18:15 (MSG) tells us: "Wise men and women are always learning, always listening for fresh insights." It's a sign of growth: "Without good direction, people lose their way; the more wise counsel you follow, the better your chances" (Proverbs 11:14 MSG). It's a sign of deepest care: "If you don't know what you're doing, pray to the Father. He loves to help. You'll get His help, and won't be condescended to when you ask for it. Ask boldly, believingly, without a second thought" (James 1:5 MSG).

Now, write this WHOLE power tool on sticky notes, poster boards, and billboards. Anywhere and everywhere you can. Keep it ever before your eyes, especially here in the beginning of our healing. As we move forward on this journey, the WHOLE power tool will become more of a reality.

HEART CARE

Reflect:
The Great Art of Not Knowing

Never be afraid to ask why. This is a gateway question that invites us into the waiting room of deeper truths; a place where we get to know God better, to know ourselves better, and to be at ease with mystery—the great art of not knowing. I take solace in the fact that even Jesus welcomed God, His Father, into His whys.

First, in a garden, hours before His journey to the cross, He prayed, not once but three times, for God to take away His suffering. From the depths of His own humanity, He cried out for relief, "My Father, if it is possible, let this cup pass from Me; yet not as I will, but as You will" (Matthew 26:39 NASB). His soul was grieved, and His heart was breaking.

And then, just minutes before His treacherous death on the cross, He cried His very last words: "'*Eli, Eli, lama sabachthani?*' which means, 'My God, my God, why have you abandoned me?'" (Matthew 27:45–46 MSG).

In the Greek, *why* simply means "for what purpose; wherefore?" Jesus knew the answer, yet He still asked why. He wanted to know "for what purpose" He was enduring such pain. Christ was fully human, fully divine. He relates to our need to understand the why behind our suffering. And yet, with His next breath, as we read in Matthew 27:50, He fully accepted and surrendered to the will of His Father. Here is the ultimate heartrift—heaven's heart torn in two. Jesus's death fulfills and offers the greatest of all heartlifts for any who accept the invitation.

The divine mystery of this reality is mind-boggling, but it displays the intersection where our faith meets reality. Jesus shows us the *hows* of moving through our *whys*. His top priority was to spend time with His Father. He modeled the vitality received from setting time apart to develop relational intimacy based on unconditional love and mutual trust. No matter what, He slipped away to check in, communicate, and care for, not only His heart but the heart of humanity as well. He had one focus—to be about His Father's business (Luke 2:49).

Reframe

One of the most important first steps in overcoming hurtful words is recognizing how and where Satan, the father of lies (John 8:44 AMP) and great enemy of our faith (1 Peter 5:8 NIV), gets a "foothold" in our lives. In Ephesians 4:25–27 (AMP), the apostle Paul helps us understand exactly what a foothold can do to us. He writes, "Therefore, rejecting all falsehood [whether lying, defrauding, telling half-truths, spreading rumors, any such as these], speak truth each one with his neighbor, for we are all parts of one another [and we are all parts of the body of Christ]. Be angry [at sin—at immorality, at injustice, at ungodly behavior], yet do not sin; do not let your anger [cause you shame, nor allow it to] last until the sun goes down. And do not give the devil an opportunity [to lead you into sin by holding a grudge, or nurturing anger, or harboring resentment, or cultivating bitterness.]"

The Amplified Bible translates *footholds* into the word "opportunity" and shows us how easily they can sneak into a life—sometimes at a very early age—and aren't recognized until we are older and made aware of their unhealthy grip on our behavior patterns. These footholds or opportunities sabotage the soul's stability, cripple our hearts with fear and intimidation, misalign the mind's thought processes, and hinder the growth of healthy behavioral patterns.

One foothold came very early in my life. I've tenderly titled it "Why the White Line?"

On my sixth birthday, as a first grader at Holy Spirit Catholic School, I had to stand on the white line that ran along the sidewalk leading to the mysterious convent. There I stood, that fateful October afternoon—knock-kneed, rocking a pair of white go-go boots in hopes of countering the starched red-checked traditional uniform—center stage for the entire school to see. Instead of playing with my friends, I stood alone. My impressionable little heart was crushed into a million pieces. If memory serves me, I was being publicly punished for talking too much in class.

I was too young to grasp what was happening at the time, but now I see clearly that a foothold entered the fabric of my soul that day, one that led to years of equating behavior with approval and acceptance, especially within the context of my faith story, as I was raised within the Catholic tradition. My sister, in the eighth grade at the time, recalls watching my peers scoff as they walked by. In response to hearing my hysterical crying, she rushed across the playground to help me. Promptly, the nuns refrained her. "It is for her good. Leave her alone."

The sting of those five words took root. *It is for her good.*

It seems that from a very young age, my inability to remain silent was an issue. God bless those nuns, but why, oh why, did they choose such a demeaning form of external punishment? I was six years old. Seriously, just take me outside and talk to me. Rarely does external punishment initiate true change. Maybe a bright red *T* should have been embroidered onto my stiff white Peter-Pan–collared blouse.

What stands out most in this memory isn't the humiliation, the embarrassment, or the sneers and snickers from the other children—even though that treatment was harsh. The most vivid memories are that I missed out on the fun and frivolity of recess and that I was all alone on that shame-filled white line.

All alone—or so I thought.

Looking through the crystal-clear lens of hindsight, perhaps God was preparing me for this very moment. He knew I was going to talk too much. He knew I was going to stand alone. He knew I might ruffle the feathers of established religious expectations (represented by the legalities of those nuns I innocently trusted), and sometimes color outside the lines. He knew I would step off the white line of expectations and restrictions, even when they were administered by people I love very much.

It seems from a very young age that the devil himself had a strong foothold in my life. I spent those formative years, when 85 percent of our personalities are developed, in the presence of strict nuns who impressed their rigidity on my tender frame.

Not only did I talk too much, I also innately wanted to do the right thing. I have very distinct memories of my dire need to please. Right then and there, I began equating obedience with being sure I toed the white line. Subconsciously, I began instructing myself not to have "too much fun." From that point forward, I worked to live according to the standards of someone else—even though those standards were *not* God's true standards for enjoying life.

Why do I share all this? Because maybe, like me, you remember a white line on your life map. A time when a person or event left an impression that perhaps changed your perception, left a dent in your sense of self, or initiated a fracture in your heart of hearts. And perhaps that moment has cast such a far-reaching shadow over your life that you still fear what could happen if you step off the white line. It's time to cast the light of truth into that darkness.

Reauthor

Storyteller Marni Gillard tells us, "We need to look hard at the stories we create, and wrestle with them. Return and retell them, and work with them like clay. It is in the retelling and returning that they give us their wisdom."[19]

Okay, are you ready? It is time to pick up your pen and begin collaborating with God to rewrite your faith story. Rewind and reset a heartrifting experience. What is your "Why the White Line" story? Is there a specific moment on your God-map where a life-changing foothold entered the scene? Peering back, I can see how the harsh tone and exacting discipline of a well-meaning Catholic nun affected me and foreshadowed the harsh tone and exacting discipline of a similarly well-meaning Protestant woman in my church. By thoroughly examining the foothold and then writing about it, I was able to process and vocalize the pain in a healthy manner, which then allowed me to press through to freedom. Ah! The heartrift fades; the heartlift comes.

Be sure to visit www.janellrardon.com for more personal stories of reframing and repairing footholds and gain even more skills for living in the freedom your heart so deeply desires.

Choose Healthy over Unhealthy

The Intention of Practice 3:
I will overcome hurtful words
by choosing healthy over unhealthy.

The one thing you can't take away from me is the way
I choose to respond to what you do to me.
The last of one's freedoms is to choose one's attitude
in any given circumstance.
—Viktor E. Frankl[20]

Today Is No Ordinary Day

Every crushed heart has a story and, as in every great story, there
is a beginning, middle, and end. Each part is critical to the whole,
but nothing is more powerful than the beginning. Great men and
women have debated the power of beginnings for centuries. Plato, the
ancient philosopher, argued that the beginning is the most important

part of any work. Screenwriter Graham Greene writes, "A story has no beginning or end: arbitrarily one chooses that moment of experience from which to look back or from which to look ahead."[21] And, British novelist Mary Shelley believed that the beginning is always today. All three of these sage minds offer keen insight, but I'm leaning toward Shelley's perspective. Today is no ordinary day. It is your day for a brand-new beginning. It is your day to take the eraser of God's love and begin overcoming unhealthy with healthy.

Every Heart Has a Beginning

Your heart had its very own beginning. From the moment you were born, it was shaped by those who held it first. The good. The bad. The ugly. A funny thing about our beginning is we had no control over it. We didn't get to choose our mothers or fathers. The early formation years are critical because, during this time, we absorb the emotional energy of our earliest caregivers. Their words (verbal), actions (nonverbal) and beliefs create an emotional atmosphere in the home, and this greatly influences our emotional development. It is in their care we learn to relate as future parents and spouses, siblings and children, workers and coworkers, congregants and citizens. We watch. We listen. We replicate. Renowned psychiatrist Dr. Bessel van der Kolk writes, "Some experiences imprint themselves beyond where language can reach."[22] These myriad connections often do imprint on our psyche and prove to be tenuous and complex. They hold an innate potential for heartbreak and hard feelings and, if we are honest, can also hold a bit of hell on earth.

Yet, when we open the pages of Genesis, the first book in the Bible, we quickly see that God felt strongly that it was "not good for the Man to be alone; I'll make him a helper, a companion" (Genesis

2:18 MSG). It seems God values relationships far more than we imagine. So much so, in fact, that He enjoyed walking and talking to the man and woman every day in the cool of the evening. But one fateful evening, Adam and Eve were nowhere to be found. God called for them: "Where are you?" Longing filled His voice as He looked forward to their time together.

But earlier that day, they had fallen prey to the lies of the enemy and done something they had been warned not to do—they had eaten the fruit of the tree in the middle of the garden. From that moment on, their relationship with God changed.

Slithering into the garden of Eden, man's first home, the enemy of God appeared to man as a serpent. No ordinary reptile, mind you, but a serpent "more crafty than any of the wild animals the LORD God had made" (Genesis 3:1). A master at the art of pretense, i.e., primping and posing, Satan's subtle tactics persuaded Eve and then Adam, her husband, to disobey God.

The Genesis of Unhealthy

Here's where we get to the beginning of unhealthy. Satan, the enemy of God, craved God's spotlight (Revelation 12:7–9). Unable to attain it, he became determined to ruin relationships, especially those built on God's beautiful, perfect love. Heartrifts are his specialty. He will do anything to ruin our relationships with God, with self, and with others. He simply can't stand it when everyone gets along. It is so important to revisit this true story, though it often seems like a fairy tale, myth, or ancient folklore. I've wrestled with including these thoughts, but it is so critical to remember that Satan and his forces are real. They are not fictional characters, like the Wicked Witch of the West, the Big Bad Wolf, or the sinister Joker who taunts Batman.

No, evil is unfortunately very real and at the heart of everything unhealthy.

As simplistic as this Eden account might sound, it reminds us of where healthy (the perfect garden) ended, and unhealthy (Adam and Eve disobey God) entered the picture. Cast from the perfect home God had created for them, Adam and Eve entered an entirely different world where they had to work, experience pain, and suffer the greatest of losses, the discomfort of disconnection from God. The moment Eve tasted the forbidden fruit, relational conflict also entered the scene. Eve blamed the serpent. Adam blamed Eve. These blaming and shaming roots reach far and wide—right into the relationships we have in our own lives today. Once naked and unashamed, Adam and Eve are now naked and ashamed. Life and everything they had known before was over.

Perhaps you feel the way I did that Saturday afternoon so long ago. Angela left me standing in a heap of emotional rubble, wondering what to do next. *Am I really as bad as she says I am? Do other women feel the way she does? Who am I, anyway?* Her piercing words made me doubt everything about myself. I wanted to call every friend I knew and ask them, "Am I a good person? Please tell me I am not as bad as she says I am. Maybe she is right. I am unworthy." Yet, I knew where I needed to go. At times like these, we must know who we are—deep on the inside. This knowledge gives us an inner strength and the secure attachment necessary to withstand the pain of hurtful words.

Our Genesis 2:7 Beginning

The first step toward a healthy heart is to travel back to where it all started—to your very own Genesis 2:7 beginning. Back to the moment in history when God decided it was time for you to be born—not a ho-hum idea, but an exacting, strategic, highly intentional decision.

Will you walk with me to that special moment?

God had created the entire earth but had not yet created anyone to take care of it. It is recorded that He "formed a man from the dust of the ground and breathed into his nostrils the breath of life, and the man became a living being" (Genesis 2:7). That same incredible, God-sized deep breath that gave life to Adam also gave life to you and me. What an astounding thought.

If I could, I'd take your hand and lead you to one of my favorite spots—a beautiful pier that extends over the historic James River near my house. I go there to catch my breath, practice being still, fill my composure tank, and oftentimes, to pray. There, we would reenact your Genesis 2:7 beginning. Over the years, I've been privileged to do this with many people—women, married couples, families, in person. Of course, we can't do that, so instead, we will do it right here, right now. Here are a few important preparations before we start:

- Find time and space. Is there a quiet place in your home, your neighborhood, your workplace, or your community where you can go to be alone? This is so important that I encourage you to get a babysitter or ask a friend for a few moments of childcare. Back in the day, I literally closed myself in the closet of our master bedroom.

- If you can, turn off all devices (unless you're reading this on one, of course).

- Settle down inside and allow the outside world to fade for a few minutes.

• Close your eyes and be mindful of this moment.

Once these critical preparations are in place, use the following meditative exercise. If you are alone, read the words below aloud with intention. If you are with a close friend or in a small group, take turns reading it aloud to one another, letting each person experience this special narrative.

Picture a beautiful, luscious garden. The colors are mesmerizing. Deer are drinking from a crystal river. Lions lie with lambs. There's a peace in the air that feels unusual, yet comforting. Gently, with grand intention, God bends down and picks up a handful of life-giving, heartlifting Eden-dust. Smiling, He closes His eyes. His mind fills with passion, purpose, potential, and endless possibilities for what is about to happen. He lifts His hand and quiets everything around Him. Silence settles in like a soft summer rain. Then He inhales, taking a God-sized deep breath, and exhales the excellence of His Being into your being. That breath of life imbues your distinct inner and outer character qualities, your gifts and talents, your purpose and passion, and gives you a God-created capacity for affecting your sphere of influence with greatness. This God-sized deep breath enables you to move through the ups and downs of life as an overcomer. When you need strength—remember this breath. When you need courage—remember this breath. When you need love—remember this breath. When you need joy—remember this breath. God's creative work is now finished. Waves of laughter and joy swell as all of Eden rejoices over your life. Hear all of heaven say, "Ah! Look at her beautiful smile. She is full of potential. God outdid Himself today."

You feel so welcome. So loved. So valued. So peaceful.

God speaks His blessing over you, His highly valued child. Then, with a heavenly embrace, He sends you off into the world to fulfill your God-breathed destiny.

Pause for a moment before continuing. Do you hear any God-whispers? Be sure to write them down. Then take yet another moment and just be. Prior to leaving, speak the following prayer aloud as the finishing touch. It is actually the text of Psalm 139:13–18, but we will speak it to God as a prayer. You will probably need your own God-sized breath—full of new vigor and faith, because this can feel foreign, especially after a season of hurt and pain. But you can invite the Comforter, your heavenly guide, to help you.

Dear God,

You created my inmost being; you knit me together in my mother's womb. I praise you because I am fearfully and wonderfully made; your works are wonderful, I know that full well. My frame was not hidden from you when I was made in the secret place, when I was woven together in the depths of the earth. Your eyes saw my unformed body; all the days ordained for me were written in your book before one of them came to be. How precious to me are your thoughts, God! How vast is the sum of them! Were I to count them, they would outnumber the grains of sand—when I awake, I am still with you. Amen.

Now, take a few moments to let it all sink deep into that beautiful soul of yours.

Letting Your Past Fortify Your Future

God knew when, where, how, and why to place you where He placed you. He placed me in California in 1959, in a home where an alcoholic father lived. I struggled with that truth for years. I desperately wanted a different story, but instead, God has helped me embrace my story.

He placed you in your specific city, in your specific year, in your specific family. Each of us are destined to live, move, and have our being in every circumstance (Acts 17:28) because we have a God-sized deep breath that enables, equips, and empowers us to overcome.

Why is acknowledging His plan for our beginning so critical? Because the day we acknowledge, understand, and surrender to this truth is the day we begin to truly live. Any trace of victim mentality will melt away, and we will begin walking as victorious people whose past now fortifies our future. Saint Catherine of Siena affirms this journey toward self-knowledge. As a young seeker, she discovered:

> Just as you can better see the blemish on your face when you look at yourself in the mirror, so the soul who in true self-knowledge rises up with desire to look at herself in the gentle mirror of God, with the eye of understanding sees all the more clearly her own defects because of the purity she sees in him. The purity of the glimpses she is getting in her moments of deep awareness is like a light that is helping her see her own imperfections—things in herself she wants to change. In the gentle mirror of God, she sees her own dignity.[23]

Self-knowledge asks us to look at our past with gentle eyes and empathic hearts. Every step of our journey leads us to greater awareness and an even greater desire to grow closer to God. The lasting pain of hurtful words becomes an inviting threshold into a new understanding of our purpose, passion, and presence here on earth.

Self-care asks us to welcome another to walk beside us. Someone to help us take the first step over the threshold. Spiritual director Dr. Alexander John Shaia reminds us how vital it is not to travel alone:

> We will absolutely require at least one human being to steady us, and more are highly recommended. The presence of wise counselors in our life cannot be underestimated, and others who are on the same path that we are, or who have traveled it ahead of us, are invaluable. Self-isolate and "go it alone" attitudes come from our fearful selves, resisting being known and changed and it is important for us to resist them back.[24]

Accepting and Understanding Our God-Created Identity

The Quaker teacher Douglas Steere was fond of saying that "the ancient human question, 'Who am I?' leads inevitably to the equally important question, 'Whose am I?' for there is no selfhood outside of relationship."[25]

There is no selfhood outside of relationship.

Accepting our Genesis 2:7 beginning means accepting our God-created identity. Once we know the source of our identity—that we are members of God's family—we will know who we are, and thus be able to fulfill our God-given capacity in every sphere of influence. Until then, we give way too much room for those unhealthy behaviors to control us. They hold us back and eventually hold back all our relationships by creating fear, fractures, and falsehood.

Identity, in its truest form, is basically that "set of characteristics by which a person or thing is definitively recognizable or known."[26]

Identity expressed:

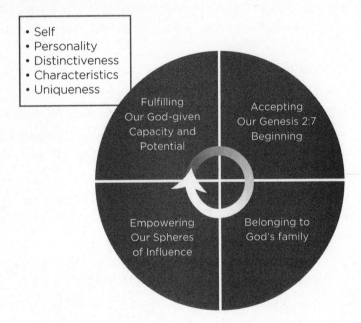

- Self
- Personality
- Distinctiveness
- Characteristics
- Uniqueness

Fulfilling Our God-given Capacity and Potential

Accepting Our Genesis 2:7 Beginning

Empowering Our Spheres of Influence

Belonging to God's family

Accepting Our Innate Need to Belong

There is great power in the verb *belong*. It isn't an easy word to define, though experts try. The *American Heritage Dictionary*, for example, defines it as "to be attached or bound by birth, allegiance, or dependency, usually used with *to*."[27] *Webster's* says it means "to be the proper concern or business of; to be part of, to be connected with, though detached in place."[28]

After mulling over this verb and searching the Scriptures, I found amazing affirmation that we do, indeed, belong completely to God. Solomon, King David's son, authored Song of Songs, the twenty-second book of the Bible, a wedding song neatly tucked between Proverbs and Isaiah. The book uses rich, descriptive language concerning love and fulfillment in the bride-bridegroom relationship. In Song of Songs 7:10 (VOICE), Solomon writes, "I belong to my love, and he has desire for me."

For me.

Two little words that deliver quite a punch. Belonging to someone, as mentioned here, brings a deep sense of safety, security, and connection. We all want to belong. We all want to feel as if we fit somewhere. This is the great secret, the moment of truth: knowing *who* we are (our God-created identity) and knowing *whose* we are (we belong to God) enables every person to be exactly who they have been created to be. Without this knowledge, we waste precious time and energy trying to be who *someone else* thinks we should be.

Expressing Our God-Created Identity

This strong, solid identification with Christ, known in counseling as "secure attachment," clarifies that, while our identities may be expressed, enhanced, and empowered by marriage partners, children, peers, culture, relationships, prosperity, politics, ambition, success, athletics, body image, service, and ministry, they will no longer be defined by them. We look to no one to define us or try to make us something we were never created to be.

The voice once hushed, the value once diminished, the victory once impeded—they emerge like a caterpillar from its cocoon. Blood has been shed, but it was necessary in order to give way to flight.

Living from this beautiful place causes pretense to fade and authenticity to flourish.

As we solidify our understanding of our God-created identity, each of us will function at our highest potential, and before you know it, we'll become heartlifters, encouraging one another to do the same. No longer will our lives be ruled by unhealthy behaviors or driven by buried emotional pain. Instead, we will be shaped by the passion to maintain healthy relationships as healthy women in healthy community. Individual healing creates community health—and that is contagious, irresistible, and freeing. It's so close I can feel it. Can you? This atmosphere of love and acceptance envelops each of us, and before you know it, it attracts others to join us on the journey.

There is nothing I want more right now than to help you grasp the power of your Genesis 2:7 beginning. To help you fully understand the power of secure attachment. When children experience secure attachment, the world is a safer, more secure place for them. Psychologist John Bowlby first coined and developed attachment theory, helping the world understand how very essential this is to living a meaningful life. When we don't experience secure attachment, we spend a great deal of emotional energy seeking security and safety. Perhaps, like me, this wasn't afforded you in your childhood. It is not too late. As you draw near to God, your heavenly Father, your capacity in this area will grow.[29]

The following Heart Care exercise might take a little while to complete. In fact, you might want to schedule an evening or overnight getaway with a close friend—or better yet, invite your trusted small group—to experience this powerful exercise. Everything you need is right here.

HEART CARE

Reflect

Eleanor Roosevelt said it best: "No one can make you feel inferior without your consent."[30] Yet, it happens. Over time, patterns can be traced that reveal positive and negative traits. This Reflect invites you to look at your history of hurts and develop your vision of victory by charting the significant markers in your life that have shaped you. Here is an excerpt from my own history of hurts that I hope will help you. Remember, I only tell my story to inform your story. Soon, you will tell your story to inform someone else's story. Healing happens in the midst of such sharing.

History of Hurts Example:
Accepting and Living My God-Created Identity

Without even being aware of it, we often look for external pursuits or people to fill our deep emotional need for understanding our value, worth, and dignity. Instead of finding these critical identity-forming qualities in my earthly father's attention and influence, it seems the competitive world of dance and beauty pageants became the basis of who I was. Without my realizing it, the stage became a foster parent of sorts. Feeling right at home under the bright lights, my identity formed under the influence of the three A's: affirmation, approval, and the addictive applause of others. Without hesitation, I remember the moment this false sense of identity entered my soul.

It was the fourth grade talent show. As I twirled my silver baton— this time successfully completing the double turn—to Galway and

Mancini's tune of "Baby Elephant Walk," I saw my peers smiling and "approving" my skills.

"How did you do that?" they asked. "You're really good."

Prior to that performance, I was the new, tall, and very lanky red-haired girl from North Carolina. After it, I was "one of them."

Over time, a web of human opinion entangled my soul, weaving an intricate pattern of pleasing others (Proverbs 29:25). Life became a cycle of standing in front of a panel of judges, much like the contestants on *Shark Tank* or *The Voice*, or standing in front of men and women in my church who seemingly held my destiny. The truth is—they didn't.

Unfortunately, this unhealthy pattern of pleasing others led me further and further away from my true, God-created identity (Genesis 2:7), which can only be found in Jesus Christ. My stage self (or world-created identity, as I like to say) took over, and the cacophony of voices crowded my thoughts and became a history of hurts. Constant criticisms filled my mind:

- Lose weight; your thighs jiggle. A tap dancer's thighs can't jiggle.
- Your evening gown looks like the upholstery of a sofa.
- Do something different with your hair.
- Study harder.
- Jog farther.
- Whiten your teeth.

Years of listening to all these voices brought me to a place of complete exhaustion. The weight of the façade finally became too heavy to bear. I had to lose unhealthy emotional weight. *Is this really what my life is all about? Why do I feel so sad all the time?* When the bright lights of the stage dimmed, the curtains closed, and the applause ceased, all that remained was a deep sense of emptiness.

Here is how I began transforming my history of hurts into a vision of victory.

The day I said, "God, part of me just wants to die," was a big day (see Practice 2). As I recollected that prayer, I realized part of me *did need* to die. Which part? The three A's: affirmation, approval, and the addictive applause of others, which I put under one roof: pretense.

I needed to value myself in order to believe in myself. I needed to both find my voice and use my voice. During this time, guiding questions arose:

- ***Why do I think the way I think?*** For me, my emotionally absent, alcoholic father had left a gaping hole in my little-girl soul. The applause and affirmation I experienced after my first public performance on stage served as a substitute for his applause and affirmation. Misshaped cognition (the thought processes in my mind) and faulty thinking (looking to others to tell me I was good and worthy of love) took root in my life instead.

- ***Why do I hear the way I hear?*** Because I lacked the nurturing bond of emotional connection with my father, I looked to others to tell me who I was. I craved their applause. This soul-emptiness hungered for attention—at any cost. Any love and attention became better than no love or attention. The absent voice of my father was replaced by the alluring—and demanding—voices of others. *Act this way. Dress this way. Live this way.*

- ***On a deeper level, why do people treat me the way they do? Why do I treat people the way I treat them?*** Sadly, my family of origin had very unhealthy communication patterns. Childhood is typically when we learn healthy communication skills: emotional regulation, conflict resolution, anger management, mood stabilization techniques, secure attachment, healthy thinking patterns, and oh, so much more. I had missed out on most of this. Thankfully, God sent great men and women into my life who guided and mentored me to health. *He will do the same for you.*

Using the simple diagram below, I charted my history of hurts.

Begin
practicing:
authenticity

Unhealthy
behavior:
pretense

Looking to
others instead of
looking to God

Accept
Genesis 2:7
Beginning

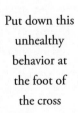

Put down this
unhealthy
behavior at
the foot of
the cross

Needing
acceptance,
approval,
applause, and
affirmation

As you look back into your history of hurts, what unhealthy behaviors kept you from becoming the remarkable woman God created you to be? You are no longer hindered by the unhealthy, but empowered with a healthy, God-created sense of value, worth, and dignity.

Now, it's your turn. Chart your own history of hurts, starting with these questions. Then, summarize and fill in your diagram below.

- Why do I think the way I do?
- Why do I hear the way I hear?
- Why do people treat me the way they do?
- Why do I treat people the way I do?

Begin
practicing:
_____

Unhealthy
behavior:
_____

What do you
look to instead of
looking to God?

Accept
Genesis 2:7
Beginning

Put down this
unhealthy
behavior at
the foot of
the cross

How does this
play out in
your daily life?

Reframe:
Creating Your Vision of Victory

Revisit the meditative exercise "Your Genesis 2:7 Beginning" (found on p. 53). Grab two 8½ x 11 sheets of paper or use a page in your journal. Draw a simple cluster diagram.

As you read through this portion of the meditative exercise, listen for God-whispers of your very own. Record your findings in the circles. Sometimes it helps to have a friend assist you with your discovery. I help women do this, and it is quite amazing. Here's a small example of my own personal discovery:

Flaming red hair, tall, lanky, very flexible, very loud voice and big laugh.

Really good at movement, fast feet for tap dancing, loves harmonizing during congregational worship, crazy about writing sensational sentences that help others.

Heartlifter. Hospitable. Intuitive. Great listener. Discerning. Creative. Strong teaching skills. Innovative.

My Genesis 2:7 Beginning

Adult child of an alcoholic. People-pleaser. Low self-esteem. Self-doubts. Perfectionist.

Helping women become remarkable. Loves to travel and meet new people. Enjoys setting a beautiful table for others to enjoy a meal.

Talks too much. Needs to learn to be quiet in order to hear God. Overachiever. Addictive behavior at times.

Reauthor

The Heart Care exercise you did in this practice has the potential to change future generations. This journey isn't just for you. It is for everyone in your sphere of influence. Spend a few quiet moments considering Proverbs 4:23 (TLB), "Above all else, guard your affections. For they influence everything else in your life." In light of all we talked about in Practice 2, what does "above all else" mean to you? What unhealthy behaviors do you want to reauthor? How can you change your narrative from negative to positive?

PART TWO: REFRAME

Past Fault Lines:
Where Is This Coming From?

Pray through and Stay with the Process

The Intention of Practice 4:
I will overcome hurtful words when I pray
through and stay with the process.

I felt like my heart had been so thoroughly and irreparably broken
that there could be no real joy again, and at best there
might eventually be a little contentment. Everyone wanted me
to get help and rejoin life, pick up the pieces and move on,
and I tried to, I wanted to, but I just had to lie in the mud
with my arms wrapped around myself, eyes closed, grieving,
until I didn't have to anymore.

—ANNE LAMOTT[31]

A Tale of Two Hearts

Open the pages of any great novel and escape into a world filled
with endless heartbreak. Whether traveling up the Congo River
with Charles Marlow (*Heart of Darkness*), imprisoned in the red

room with *Jane Eyre*, meeting Victor Frankenstein in the icy Arctic (*Frankenstein*), or fleeing from a royal ball before the clock strikes midnight (*Cinderella*), novelists give words to our deepest fears, our deepest longings, and our deepest desires. Somehow, the power of story transcends time, culture, and history. It wields an immense, uncanny power and ability, unlike any other medium. It grabs our hearts and gives voice to the voiceless, life to the lifeless, and hope to the hopeless. But no story offers entrance into the world of relationships like the greatest story ever told—the Bible. Full of romance, conflict, betrayal, and the ultimate triumph of good over evil, these true stories reveal the power of real love working out in the lives of real people. People just like you and me.

Somewhere in the midst of moving through the healing process of my own crushing, I found a story in the Old Testament that literally changed my life. A profound statement, yes, but very true. I've held my Bible close to my heart for years, but it seemed to come alive for me during this traumatic time. They say desperate times call for desperate measures. I needed this ancient text to speak, and it did. From a quiet, often overlooked chapter in my Bible, a voice of wisdom called out. First Samuel 1 contains a tale of two hearts and is filled with lessons on both healthy and unhealthy behaviors. If the cameras of reality TV had been rolling in 1083 BC, these two women would have been catapulted into stardom, starring in *The Real Housewives of Ephraim* or perhaps guest stars on an episode of *Sister Wives*.

Meet Peninnah (we'll call her Penni): the *seeming* antagonist.

Meet Hannah: the protagonist.

Imagine the frenzy social media would have had with this juicy storyline. Hannah's cover on *People* Magazine might read: "Poor

Hannah—Unable to Give Her Husband a Beloved Firstborn Son." Or maybe "Elkanah Uses Surrogate to Give Him Children." Tweets might have read, "Motherhood is hopeless for Hannah. Bring on the next woman!" And if the shame of infertility wasn't enough, Elkanah's second wife, Peninnah—who was fertile beyond fertile—relentlessly flaunted that fertility daily. Might a conversation like this have taken place?

"Hey, Hannah," shouted Penni. "Ready to go to church?"

"Yes, just a second." Hannah sighed. "Let me get my things." *Another Sabbath. Another long walk to the temple. Every pounding step matched with Penni's relentless, pounding commentary.*

"Oh, look at little Elkie!" Penni giggled. "Doesn't he look just like his father? That little dimple in his chin . . . just like him. And Josiah—that cowlick . . . mirror image of Elkanah. Aren't they adorable, Hannah?"

The familiar knife cut straight through Hannah's heart and barren womb. Years of infertility hung over her head like a looming storm cloud.

"Lord," Hannah prayed under her breath. "Why does she have to be like that? What have I ever done to her? She knows I can't get pregnant, and yet she flaunts her flock of children right in front of me . . . every Sabbath. What I wouldn't give for just one little boy to love."

"Oh, Hannah," Penni said with a smirk. "Can you please run after little Ezra—he's getting way ahead of us. I can't keep up with all these children. They're going to be the death of me yet!"

Taking a long, deep breath of silent pain, Hannah scooped up Ezra, nestling his chubby little two-year-old frame into her arms, as if he was her own.

"One day, Lord; I know," she prayed yet again, the quiver in her voice steadied by a deeper trust. "One day."

The Mystery of the "Mean or Well-Meaning" Question

For several years, I traced Hannah's painful struggles with Penni. Hannah became very real to me, not just a Bible character on a page in an ancient book. Her story seemed to parallel my own. Her ability to overcome hurtful words showed me how to overcome my own hurtful words. And now, I hope it helps you to do the same. Even though this story took place centuries ago, it still rings true today. Hannah had to overcome hurtful words—without the resources and tools available to us today—but she did it. We can do it too.

We aren't given much to work with, only twenty-eight verses, so I turned to theologians, Bible commentators, and a handful of authors who had also tried to figure out this relationship. With intensity and a strong desire to see every angle of the account, I looked at Penni's side of the story. It is important to be open-minded in order to gain insights from the other person's perspective.

The contentious relationship between Elkanah's wives begs the hard question, "Is this woman, Penni, well-meaning or just plain mean?" We can only discern the mystery of these two thoughts, mean or well-meaning, when we look at the words inside the words. We can place them side by side and see how different they are:

Mean (adjective)[32]	Well-Meaning (adjective)[33]
1. Offensive, selfish, or unaccommodating.	1. Having good intentions.
2. Small-minded [having narrow interests, sympathies, or outlook— marked by pettiness, narrowness, or meanness.]	What is an intention? An act or instance of determining *mentally* upon some action or result.

I desperately tried to give Penni the benefit of the doubt. She didn't have it easy. She lived in the backdrop of Elkanah's deep, openly favored love for Hannah. *That had to hurt.* She bore the responsibility of taking care of Elkanah's children—while Hannah enjoyed less responsibility and a more pleasurable life. *That must have been frustrating.* Finally, she lived in the role of runner-up. In the words of race-car driver Dale Earnhardt, "Second place is first loser." *Ouch.*

But when it was all said and done, there was no sugarcoating Penni's unhealthy, hurtful presence in Hannah's life. The evidence is clear: "Because the LORD had closed Hannah's womb, her rival kept provoking her in order to irritate her" (1 Samuel 1:6). Penni was Hannah's rival. Plain and simple, she was not a nice person.

None of us ever want to believe that someone is mean-spirited. We offer endless excuses for the mean behavior of others, sometimes at grave expense, desperately trying to believe the best. But there are mean people in this world who deliberately hurt with their words. Sometimes we play a part in the scenario; sometimes we are just relational casualties. Time after time, I listen to similar stories from my clients. Through weary and worn-down whispers, they speak. *I've been so hurt. Why is she so mean to me? I can't forgive her for what she did to me. Why me? How can she act that way and call herself a Christian woman?* I sit in disbelief and grief. Over and over again, women share how they melt down under the mystery of mean women.

What do we do, then, when we can't escape or hide or get away from our antagonists? I believe Hannah's response to Penni's relentless pounding shows us the hows, whys, and whats of praying through and staying with all the perplexing pain of hurtful words.

In the midst of her bruised and broken heart, Hannah had some important decisions to make. She could fight against Penni. She could be catty and deliberately hurtful in her own remarks; she could be spiteful. She could retaliate by verbally attacking Penni like Penni did her. After all, an eye for an eye, right? She could play the blame game and blame Penni for everything. Or she could gossip about Penni to the other women in their community—mar her character and create a dark shadow around her. Maybe she could wail and scream and plead that Elkanah punish Penni for her mean words and actions.

She could even isolate herself and sink into a deep, dark hole of despair; possibly end it all. She could allow a serious heartrift to hamper her life and future. She could say to heck with it all and run away from her family, children, and community. But she didn't.

Fighting for the Whole World to See

Thankfully, Hannah didn't have social media to deal with. We, on the other hand, do. This new digital landscape offers even more opportunity to wield hurtful words—and it is done in front of the whole world. We've watched this play out between our best friends, feuding celebrities, and even government officials. It's never a pretty sight.

Tweets that tear down. Snapchats that deride. Violent videos that go viral. And why not Facebook Live it all—while it is happening?

Suddenly, everybody's business is everybody's business. The social filter is gone, the veil of etiquette and common courtesy torn as we let words fly without looking into the eyes of the other person. Cruel, derogatory words, typed while cowardly hiding behind screens, serve a one-two punch and, more often than not, throw the ultimate knock-out. The sad part is, nobody wins. Everybody loses. The currency of hurtful words leaves everyone in a state of emotional debt.

Keeping all of this in mind, I couldn't help but wonder how Hannah would navigate this new digital danger zone. I found myself reading and rereading every line of her ancient story, trying to unlock her secrets for the here and now. I needed her to talk to me, to show me how to pray through and stay with the process without losing my mind. I'd think of a question, write it down in my journal, and pray for answers.

- How did she keep going in the face of such harsh treatment? (1 Samuel 1:6–7)
- How and why did she stay? (1 Samuel 1:5)
- How did she refrain from retaliation? (1 Samuel 1:10)
- What did she know about loving others? (1 Samuel 1:10–12)
- What kept her from going absolutely crazy? (1 Samuel 1:12–18)

The Power of a Little Conjunction

I found my answer nestled in the middle of the story. First Samuel 1:10 (ESV) says it all: Hannah "was deeply distressed and prayed to the Lord and wept bitterly." Never before has the conjunction *and* meant so much. Leave it out and the sentence reads: Hannah wept bitterly. Add it back and *voilà!* Hannah prayed to the Lord *and* wept bitterly. Hannah had two choices before her: one choice would leave her depressed and distressed. The other choice would lead her to overcome Penni's hurtful words. If Hannah stayed in the weeping state, she would stay stuck in her heartrift. If she could find her way to the praying and staying state, she would rise above the pain of her antagonist and eventually experience the exhilarating, lasting freedom of a heartlift.

How did she actually overcome Penni's hurtful words? The same way we will: one brave whisper-prayer at a time—*God help me.*

Even Eli the priest misread Hannah. He thought she was a drunken woman (1 Samuel 1:13). From his reaction, we can assume she appeared out of her mind, but was she? Or had she entered into what spiritual director Richard Foster calls "spiritual ecstasy"?[34]

Her never-ending struggle had left her listless, stripped of self-sufficiency, and totally dependent on the God she knew and loved. Dr. James W. Goll, president of God Encounters Ministries, notes, "To an outside observer, someone caught up in the realm of the Spirit and taken to a rapturous place may appear drunk. The essence of this experience is to be overwhelmed by God's presence."[35] Hannah, overwhelmed in the spirit, prayed through and stayed with her crisis until she got to the other side of it. She didn't let it ruin her; she let it raise her to a higher level of spiritual maturity.

While sitting in a café reading these words, I closed my eyes and prayed for a faith like Hannah's. She seemed to be so intimately acquainted and securely attached to her God. Their relationship reached way beyond the walls of a weekly worship service and deep into the hallowed hallways of her home. Hannah didn't have Google

Apps to calm her nerves, Siri to search for answers, or weekly Bible studies and prayer meetings (that we know of). We have no record of close companions who walked this journey with her. At the end of the day, it was Hannah and God.

In *Plan B: Further Thoughts on Faith*, author Anne Lamott writes, "There's a lovely Hasidic story of a rabbi who always told his people that if they studied the Torah, it would put Scripture on their hearts. One of them asked, 'Why on our hearts, and not in them?' The rabbi answered, 'Only God can put Scripture inside. But reading sacred text can put it on your heart, and then when your heart breaks, the holy words will fall inside.'"[36]

In the midst of Hannah's pain, holy words fell inside her heart.

Perhaps this is *why* Hannah's journey resonated so deeply. She had nothing and no one, but God, to turn to. As we've so clearly seen, it was Hannah and her God. Period. All creature comforts stripped away. Her only hope was that God would be true to His word.

Much like Hannah, our heartrifting journeys leave us with one place to turn: *God and God alone* (Psalm 16:5)—and "alone" can be a very scary place—but Hannah's courage gave me courage. Her faith gave me even greater faith. The holy words of Deuteronomy 31:8 (NLT) had fallen inside her heart, "Do not be afraid or discouraged, for the LORD will personally go ahead of you. He will be with you; he will neither fail you nor abandon you."

May these powerful words fall inside our hearts, right now.

Praying and Staying Power Leads to Remarkable Resilience

Years passed for me, with 1 Samuel 1:10 rolling around in my mind. The more I thought about that powerful little conjunction, the more

I realized it was the secret weapon in rising above the crushing pain of hurtful words. Could Hannah have run away? I wondered. I'm not sure that was even an option for her. Sometimes, it isn't. So often the lasting pain of hurtful words comes from people we can't run away from. They are in our families or communities or churches or workplaces. They aren't going anywhere, and we haven't been released to go either.

But whatever the case, Hannah hadn't been released. She had to stay in her crushed state for a very long time. Her only alternative? To pray through and stay with the process.

Stay is an interesting word. Derived from the Latin root *stare*, it literally means "to stand." Take a look:

Stay (Intransitive Verb)[37]	Stay (Noun)[38]
1. To stand firm. 2. To sustain or strengthen mentally or spiritually; to rest on something for support. 3. To stick or remain with (as a race or trial of endurance) to the end—usually used in the phrase *stay the course*.	1. A capacity for endurance. 2. A sojourn or temporary residence.

Hannah stayed the course and, in doing so, was both sustained and strengthened, mentally and spiritually. To anyone looking through the natural eye at Hannah's life, it would appear she was physically wasting away—fatigued and frail on the outside. Yet, if we look through spiritual eyes, we would see her capacity for endurance was being enlarged. She was becoming, as we say today, "a bigger, better person."

Clinical psychologist and author Robert J. Wicks defines this staying and praying power as *spiritual resilience*:

> Spiritual resilience is not simply about recovering from adversity. It is about bouncing back in a way that deeper knowledge of both God and self may result. With the right guidance, during difficult times and periods of confusion, pain, and stress, we have a unique opportunity to nurture our relationship with God and enable it to grow in surprising ways.[39]

Hannah's Relentless Pursuit of Love

Hannah's spiritual resilience empowered her to pursue love with relentless spiritual energy. Nothing Penni did was going to stop her from seeking God. When Penni pushed her down, Hannah pressed in, harder and harder. In her private, personal pain, she somehow discovered the antidote to succumbing to the oppressor—the deep, mysterious, life-altering love of God.

This is not a love she knew before. Even though it is obvious she was deeply loved by Elkanah, her husband, his love was not enough for Hannah. He even asked, "Hannah, why are you weeping? Why don't you eat? Why are you downhearted? Don't I mean more to you than ten sons?"

Hannah's response to her husband is nowhere to be found in Scripture, but it does say she continued weeping bitterly and praying.

She continued seeking the love of her God. It seems she replied without saying, "No, Elkanah, you are not enough." Again, at the end of the day, it was Hannah and God. There is no doubting Elkanah's love for his first wife; we're told he loved her very much. But I'm beginning to believe there are times in each of our lives where human love will fail us—even the deep love of those in our most intimate relationships. This is no reflection on their ability to love or comfort us; it is, perhaps, more a reflection of God's desire to draw us closer to Himself. One of my favorite Bible commentators, F. B. Meyer, writes, "When we've come to the end of ourselves, we come to the beginning of God."[40]

Do the One Thing
that Changes Everything

In the midst of her painful heartrift, Hannah did the one thing that could change everything—she chose love over hate. I don't believe this was an easy choice for her. It rarely is. Something tells me that is why she stayed so long in the weeping state. Hate is a real emotion. It's hard to ignore. We face it, fight it, and finish the work until the *feeling* of hate is ultimately overwhelmed by God's love. Hannah knew that fighting mean with mean would create an ugly scene—in her heart and her home—so she put off the temptation to react and retaliate (unhealthy) and instead decided to practice love (healthy). Hannah knew that relationships can only change when we put into practice the words written and recorded in the ancient text of God's Word.

Centuries after Hannah lived, one man, the apostle Paul, wrote several letters about *how* to love. Part of me wants to believe that Paul read the ancient scrolls of Hannah's story and drew his writings on this subject from her life. We'll never know. It does seem that 1 Corinthians 13:1–13 (NLT) describes her actions to a T:

If I could speak all the languages of earth and of angels, but didn't love others, I would only be a noisy gong or a clanging cymbal. If I had the gift of prophecy, and if I understood all of God's secret plans and possessed all knowledge, and if I had such faith that I could move mountains, but didn't love others, I would be nothing. If I gave everything I have to the poor and even sacrificed my body, I could boast about it; but if I didn't love others, I would have gained nothing.

Love is patient and kind. Love is not jealous or boastful or proud or rude. It does not demand its own way. It is not irritable, and it keeps no record of being wronged. It does not rejoice about injustice but rejoices whenever the truth wins out. Love never gives up, never loses faith, is always hopeful, and endures through every circumstance.

Prophecy and speaking in unknown languages and special knowledge will become useless. But love will last forever! Now our knowledge is partial and incomplete, and even the gift of prophecy reveals only part of the whole picture! But when the time of perfection comes, these partial things will become useless.

When I was a child, I spoke and thought and reasoned as a child. But when I grew up, I put away childish things. Now we see things imperfectly, like puzzling reflections in a mirror, but then we will see everything with perfect clarity. All that I know now is partial and incomplete, but then I will know everything completely, just as God now knows me completely.

Three things will last forever—faith, hope, and love—
and the greatest of these is love.

Hannah Left a Rich Legacy
of Authentic Love

More than anything, Hannah led me to understand that life is not
about advancing the kingdom of self; it is about advancing the kingdom of God. Her decision to love rather than hate was how she
finally overcame the hurtful words of her antagonist. As difficult as
this seems, I am here to say it can happen. Hannah taught me to
pray through and stay with the process until God gave me His love
for Angela. Honestly, I never *hated* Angela. I was deeply grieved at
the strain and unhealthy nature of our relationship. The aftermath re-
quired a great deal of me. I had to process this grief—moving through
each of the five stages, slowly. I sought wise counsel. I spent a great
deal of time on my own heart care. I finished my Master's work and
prayed more than I ever have. As mature women and followers of
Christ, we simply didn't have healthy tools in our emotional and
relational toolbox. Because of this, my passion for helping myself
and other women get these tools was born. I promised myself that I
would do everything in my power to share Hannah's three-fold cord
of authentic love with everyone I could:

- *Authentic love looks upward to God.* Personal redemption
  comes at the foot of the cross (John 3:16). It is hard to accept
  that Jesus died for you and me, but He did. Feel His hand
  lifting your chin. Hear His voice calling your name. Hold His
  hand as He leads you forward. There is no greater love in all
  the world than God's love for you. In that very scary "alone"

place with God, love will come. I promise. Pray through and stay with the process until it does.

- *Authentic love looks inward to the heart.* It is utterly impossible to deeply love another human being without first receiving love from God (see 1 Corinthians 2; Ephesians 1). I know that God can and will give you love. He has done this for me, and He will do it for you. It is a miracle, yes, but we have a miracle-giving God.

- *Authentic love looks outward to others.* Once received, we offer this gift and grace to others (see 1 John 2:1–11). We cannot keep this God-given love to ourselves. It is impossible. It will overflow to everyone in our sphere of influence. Authentic love also discerns that loving others will, at times, look like walking away, setting healthy boundaries, or speaking the truth in love. Even Paul, the author of the biblical love chapter reprinted above, knew that getting along with everyone is virtually impossible. He wrote, "If it is possible, as far as it depends on you, live at peace with everyone" (Romans 12:18). There will be times when we will have to agree to disagree.

In simplest terms, our ability to love always begins in the heart—it's the center of all physical and spiritual life (see 1 Peter 1:22). It is the all-important why behind the need to take care of our own hearts.

To help my clients move forward on their heartlift journeys, I've created simple illustrations that help them identify what might be hindering their capacity to overcome hurtful words. Take a moment to look at each.

Upon your first glance at Figure 1, one word/negative behavior will jump out at you. Trust your instinct detector. Go with the very first word that stands out. Either circle the word or write it in the margin. In the Heart Care section, we will dig deeper into this exercise. (I often wonder what Hannah and Penni might "see" upon first glance. Might Hannah choose depression? Might Penni choose envy/jealousy/comparison, the triplets of relational aggression?) Now, it's your turn. What might be hindering you from overcoming? We've identified my downfall: people pleasing.

Next, glance at Figure 2. What healthy virtue reframes your unhealthy, heartrifting behavior? For example, security reframes people pleasing.

Figure 1. The crushed heart: unhealthy, heartrifting behaviors

Figure 2. The whole heart: healthy, heartlifting behaviors

In doing this exercise, we examine our hearts and look into the mirrors of our behavior, speech, and interpersonal relationships (see James 1:22–25). As we answer the call to lay aside our egos, personal ambition, and striving—agreeing to disagree when it comes to some issues—and face the reality and presence of relational aggression—including such unhealthy behaviors as jealousy, envy, comparison, insecurity, inferiority, gossip, rumor, controlling personalities, fa-çade, and oppressive attitudes—we will ultimately learn to respond through the gifts of repentance, reconciliation, and restoration. When we practice these vital principles, real change can and will happen.

HEART CARE

Reflect

Hannah sets the bar high. It seems she truly exhibits the "E" of our WHOLE power tool. She elevates the atmosphere time and time again. Penni's raging fault lines didn't hit just once. First Samuel 1:7 says, "This went on year after year. Whenever Hannah went up to the house of the LORD, her rival provoked her till she wept and would not eat." Imagine how many times she had to whisper, *God help me.*

Take a few moments to read through 1 Corinthians 13:1–13 again. Check out several versions on www.biblegateway.com or www.biblestudytools.com and consider the following questions:

- How on earth is this type of love even possible? (See 1 John 4:19–20.)
- Take time to remember when you first received the message of God's love. How did it change your heart? How did it change your life? How did it change your relationships?
- What does this redeeming love of God look like on a daily basis? In your home? In your family? In your community? In your church?

Reframe

We will continue to look at Hannah's life and her relationship with Penni. For right now, let's consider two short Scriptures:

- 1 Samuel 1:10 (ESV): "She was deeply distressed and prayed to the LORD and wept bitterly."

- 1 Samuel 1:15: "I am a woman who is deeply troubled. I have not been drinking wine or beer; I was pouring out my soul to the LORD."

These two verses might be short, but they are filled with insight and wisdom into how and where she found the capacity to love. Record your thoughts here or in your journal. Consider:

- Hannah's relationship to God
- Hannah's understanding of prayer
- Hannah's emotional state
- Hannah's capacity to receive from God
- Hannah's belief system

In light of this short study, consider:

- Your relationship to God
- Your understanding of prayer
- Your emotional state
- Your capacity to receive from God
- Your belief system

Reauthor

Revisit the hearts in Figures 1 and 2. Remember the two words you either circled or wrote in the margin? Complete this meditative exercise:

- Grab two sheets of paper, some colored pencils or markers, a dictionary, a Bible, and a Bible concordance. If you have access to the Internet, use www.blueletterbible.com or www.biblegateway.com.

- Write the word you chose from Figure 1 in the middle of one piece of paper and the word you chose from Figure 2 on the other piece of paper.

- Define each.

- Then, using your Bible concordance, search for Scriptures that use this word. Choose three to five verses that stand out to you. Write these words on the papers surrounding the main word.

- Take your time. You don't have to do both word studies at once.

I've included two samples for you.

GRUDGE
Hebrew: natar
to guard; figuratively,
to cherish anger.

Grudge defined:

"To be discontented at another's enjoyments or advantages; to envy one the possession or happiness which we desire for ourselves." (Websters, 1828.)

Give up the
GRUDGE.

Grudge not one against another, brethren, lest ye be condemned; behold, the judge standeth before the door. —James 5:9 (KJV)

GOD IS SHEER MERCY AND GRACE; NOT EASILY ANGERED; HE'S RICH IN LOVE. He doesn't endlessly nag and scold; nor hold grudges forever. He doesn't treat us as our sins deserve, nor pay us back in full for our wrongs. As high as heaven is over the earth, so strong is his love to those who fear him. And as far as sunrise is from sunset, he has separated us from our sins. —Psalm 103:6–12 (MSG)

Do not nurse hatred in your heart for any of your relatives. Confront people directly so you will not be held guilty for their sin. Do not seek revenge or bear a grudge against a fellow Israelite, but love your neighbor as yourself. I am the LORD. —Leviticus 19:17–18 (NLT)

Love (n) defined:

"An affection of the mind excited by beauty and worth of any kind, or by the qualities of an object which communicate pleasure, sensual or intellectual. It is opposed to hatred."
(Websters, 1828).

LOVE
Greek: agape
affection, good will, benevolence, brotherly love.

Live out the

LOVE.

A new commandment I give you: Love one another. As I have loved you, so you must love one another. —John 13:34

Above all, love each other deeply, because love covers over a multitude of sins.
—*1 Peter 4:8* (NIV)

LOVE IS PATIENT AND KIND. Love is not jealous or boastful or proud or rude. It does not demand its own way. It is not irritable, and it keeps no record of being wronged. It does not rejoice about injustice, but rejoices whenever the truth wins out. Love never gives up, never loses faith, is always hopeful, and endures through every circumstance.
—*1 Corinthians 13:4–7* (NLT)

PRACTICE 5

Collect Strength

The Intention of Practice 5:
I will overcome hurtful words when
I collect strength in the reservoir of my soul.

For one human being to love another; that is perhaps
the most difficult of all tasks, the ultimate,
the last test and proof, the work for which all other work
is but preparation. I hold this to be the highest task
for a bond between two people; that each protects
the solitude of the other. This is the miracle
that happens every time to those who really love:
the more they give, the more they possess.
—Rainer Maria Rilke[41]

The smell of incense filled the entire sanctuary. Nestled in the crook of my mother's right arm, I sat in the silence. A curious, sensitive eight-year-old . . . wondering, watching, and waiting. One by one, men and women approached the priest, whose round face was kind and welcoming. With great care, he dipped his right index finger into a golden bowl of black ashes. Slowly and methodically, he leaned in, creating a small black cross on each forehead.

"Remember, man, that 'dust thou art, and unto dust shalt thou return'" [Genesis 3:19 KJV], he whispered, carefully looking at each person standing in front of him as if they were the only person in the world. I imagined that must be how Jesus, the man I heard the priest talking about, must have looked at the people standing in front of Him. One by one, they brought their hearts, their pain, and their great need to Him. They wanted His blessing. His validation.

He, too, must have kind and welcoming eyes, I thought.

I didn't understand what was going on in that special candle-light service, but I felt calm and safe. I listened closely to the words and prayers being spoken—the somber tone, the cadence of background chants being sung by the choir, and the ethereal presence of something so much bigger than the sanctuary we were sitting in. I watched those around me closely—prayer hands tucked under their chins, eyes closed, and heads bowed. Some seemed to be talking, but no words were coming out of their mouths.

Looking back, I now understand what I was seeing. What I was sensing. What I was savoring. *Connection.* These men and women, the priest, my mother—they were connected to *something* and *Someone* I knew nothing about but deeply desired to discover. I didn't know to call it spirituality, sacred space, or seeking. I just knew that inside this place we called church—a place I knew as a refuge—God seemed real and very close.

A Heart Needs Rest

Very often, heartrifts fire intense relational strain and bring prolonged periods of heightened emotional stress. Even if we dismiss them on the surface, their embers radiate deep within. Moments turn into months, and months can turn into years—much like Hannah experienced with Penni. The weight of heavy and hurtful words weighs us down and leads to emotional depletion. Raised adrenaline in the bloodstream equals raised anxiety.

One in ten Americans currently takes an antidepressant—but for women in their forties and fifties, this figure jumps to one in four.[42] In our hyperconnected, digitally demanding, social-networked society, we forget that our bodies have physical limits and, more importantly, our hearts have emotional limits.

There is no emotional reserve, *yet there must be*.

Rest = Collecting Strength

So often when we think of rest, we envision long winter naps, extended vacations at a health spa, or even better, time alone on an island—book in one hand, fruited drink with a cute little umbrella in the other. If I am honest, which I always try to be, I used to think of rest as something for underachievers. Dare I say, slackers?

I was wrong. Peel back the layers of the true meaning of the word *rest*, and you'll find it literally means "recovering or collecting strength." Rest, or *anapauo* in Greek, means, "to cause or permit one to cease from any movement or labor in order to recover and collect one's strength."[43] Two powerful truths seem to shine through here.

First, to *permit* means "to give authorization or consent to someone to do something."[44] Author Brené Brown, in her book *Rising Strong*, shares how she wrote her first permission slip when she was on Oprah's *Super Soul Sunday*. The fear she experienced led her to give herself written "permission to be excited, have fun, and be goofy."[45]

That seemingly senseless, spontaneous little scribble allowed her to be herself. Sometimes we have to write ourselves permission slips, don't we? Literally authorize and give consent to take time to recover and collect strength. It sounds so ridiculous on paper, but is so true. Since hearing her story, I've written hundreds for myself—things like

Permission to set healthy boundaries with emotionally unhealthy people.
Permission to not agree with someone for the sake of keeping the peace.
Permission to speak my mind.
Permission to say no when pressured to say yes.
Permission to stop shaming myself.
Permission to practice self-compassion.

Second, we give ourselves permission to rest in order to recover and collect strength. This is the heart of the matter (pun intended). The phrase "in order to" is classified as a subordinating conjunction, poised to stress the importance and purpose of something. Here, it stresses the importance of rest *in order to* collect strength. When we give ourselves permission to collect strength, we can move through life from a healthy place and at a healthy pace. Fractured and frazzled becomes calm and centered—well balanced and serene.

The day I started saying out loud, "I need to collect strength," and actually began to make it a daily practice, was a game changer. I haven't looked back since. I've taken *rest* out of my personal vocabulary and instead use *collecting strength*. The visual and sensory imagery it evokes in my mind prods my thoughts in a whole new direction and somehow makes it easier to schedule on my calendar.

I suppose it helps me write those permission slips I need. There are times I can actually feel my rest tank start to lean toward empty. When this happens, fatigue settles in, emotional strain rises, and my capacity to operate from my healthy place weakens. I get cranky and very tense.

Solitude Invites Us to Connect

One of my favorite literary giants, Anne Morrow Lindbergh, in her famed *Gift from the Sea*, said it best. "Women need solitude in order to find again the true essence of themselves."[46] Here is a woman, living in the 1950s, writing herself a permission slip to collect strength. Once a year, Anne and her sister traveled to Captiva Island where together they shed all of their cares and responsibilities for the peace and calm of beach life. Seven, sometimes fourteen, whole days away from it all. (Before you say, "I could never do that," please read on. We are going to make this happen in our lives. I promise.)

Taking this much time away was no easy feat for Anne. She was the wife of famed transatlantic American aviator Charles Lindbergh, mother to five children, and a woman of significant status in her community and the nation. Yet, she and Charles knew that in order for Anne to be her very best self, she needed time to recover and collect her strength. She added,

> It is not physical solitude that separates one from other men, not physical isolation, but spiritual isolation. When one is a stranger to oneself, then one is estranged from others too. If one is out of touch with oneself, then one cannot touch others. Only when one is connected to one's own core is one connected to others, I am beginning to discover. And, for

me, the core, the inner spring, can best be found through solitude.[47]

There's that word again, *connected*. From the Latin root *conectere*: *con*, meaning "together," and *nectere,* meaning "bind."[48] We see here another image of the threefold cord Solomon wrote about in Ecclesiastes 4:12—the one not easily broken. Our connection to God, connection to self, and connection to others can form such a bond. Solitude invites us to connect on all three levels. It also invites us to disconnect and to examine how we use our time and energy.

I used to think this desire for solitude was selfish. In fact, many well-meaning women told me it was selfish. I booked a hotel room at a retreat one time—a room all by myself—and many misunderstood my need for solitude. *This is a time for community building. You should stay with someone who doesn't have anyone. It's not about you, Janell.*

Now I know better. There is such a tension here. Sometimes it *is* about us. At the time, I was a homeschooling mom of very active children. Every day was spent at maximum capacity. I truly needed rest. Times of solitude are all about self-care and self-preservation. If I don't take care of the three most important people in my life—me, myself, and I—in the healthiest way possible, I am no good to anyone. For years, I was told that the Christian way of life was spelled J-O-Y: Jesus, Others, You. My teachers were lovely, earnest, ardent followers of Jesus. They truly believed what they were teaching. I did too.

Until I didn't.

After my first book, *Rock-Solid Families*, was published, I met hundreds of women and listened intently to their stories. We opened a grand conversation about the heart of our families. We stopped long enough to check the pulse of our homes. Asked, "How are we doing as wives? Moms? Women?" One after another, women shared with me their private pain, many through tears of great sadness. I began to notice a sincere lack of joy. I began to hear similar stories. Individual sighs became one great communal groan. The discontent percolating deep within their hearts was so alarming that I actually put down my writing pen. At fifty years old, I took a huge leap of faith and went back to school to pursue a master's degree in counseling. I needed more tools in my own toolbox.

During this time, Monica, a woman I'd met in one of my seminars, rang my doorbell. She was seeking a safe place to land. Somewhere to sift through years of heartrifts. She was lost, lonely, and listless. Monica needed a heartlift.

She walked in, stood in the foyer, and took a deep breath. Within minutes, she'd melted into the oversized leather chair in my office. Her nonverbals said it all. Shoulders slumped. Furrowed brow. Weary eyes. She became a puddle of tears.

"I'm so exhausted. Sooooo done. I can't take any more." She paused to dig her pinging phone out of her purse. "Why won't they leave me alone? Just for a minute! I want to throw this phone in the trash. I never get one minute's peace."

"Monica, give me your phone." She handed it to me, and I set it to silent. Muted the manic messages. "They can live without you for sixty minutes. If they can't, they will quickly learn how."

We have a saying in my practice: Is this a one-tissue, three-tissues, or (when it is a really bad day) a whole-box-of-tissues day? Whatever the case, I always have a fresh box of tissues ready and waiting.

Trying to lighten Monica's heart, I placed the beautiful white tissue holder with "Breathe" etched in silver on its front right next to her. "It looks like it might be a ten-tissue day."

"I think I might need the whole box—all ninety-six tissues," she said while sniffling. Then she said something I'll never forget. With her head cradled in her hands, her voice muffled, she cried out, "I should be able to handle all of this. Seriously, there are people in the world that have way more going on than I do. Why can't I handle my life? What is wrong with me?"

Monica's heart spoke loud and clear that day. Flooded by strong, overwhelming emotions and a whole lot of people shaming and *shoulding* all over her, her heart was screaming for some much-needed rest. Shoulding is something I am quite allergic to these days. A kissing cousin of judging, it lays a heavy burden on its recipient. She mentioned some of those expectations:

- Her mother: "You should ask Nancy to help you with time management. She's always been the organized one in the family."
- Her sister: "You should learn to say no. The reason you are so exhausted is because you always try to do too much."
- Her friend: "You should call me more often. You never make time for me."
- Her neighbor: "You should get control of your children. I have these great parenting tapes you can borrow."
- Her church: "You should bring your children to Wednesday night Bible club. They need to be here."

"Monica," I said, "you are right about one thing. Yes, you are done. Done with putting everyone else first. Done with faulty thinking. Done with blurry boundaries. Done drowning in a sea of shaming and shoulding voices. It is time to practice some self-love and self-compassion."

Love Myself? Isn't That Selfish?

Why do we have such a hard time loving ourselves? Not the selfish, narcissistic kind of self-love, but a caring-for-our-own-emotional-and-mental-health kind of love. We put everyone else first. It is expected of us. At least, that is what we expect of ourselves. Every time I sit on an airplane and listen to the attendant tell me to put on my oxygen mask first, I wince. Until my recent revelation of self-care, I would have ignored the message, and I would have gotten annoyed at the messenger. Today, with no hesitation, I would put on the oxygen mask first. If I am not healthy and strong myself, I can't help anybody else.

Monica made me realize that somewhere along the way, we have misconstrued the words of Jesus as recorded in Mark 12:28–32 (TLB). Someone asked Jesus a pointed question: "Of all the commandments, which is the most important?" Jesus answered, "The one that says, 'Hear, O Israel! The Lord our God is the one and only God. And you must love him with all your heart and soul and mind and strength.' The second is: 'You must love others as much as yourself.' No other commandments are greater than these."

Love, in both of these instances, is *agape* love, meaning "to welcome, to entertain, to be fond of, to love dearly."[49] Ah! Agape. That beautiful word that invites us to sit down and just be. Agape creates a sense of peace and presence. No misplaced expectations, no shoulding, shaming, or hidden agendas. Agape lights a candle, sets a beautiful table, and says, "Come."

Agape also begs us to look inside our hearts and ask ourselves some intimate questions:

- Am I well pleased and contented with myself? Am I fond of or do I dearly love myself? Do I consider myself beloved— a much-loved person?
- Do I derive my love of self from others?
- Do I derive my love of self from my achievements, accolades, or outward appearance?
- Do I derive my love of self from anything outside of an inner knowledge that "in Christ and Christ alone, I have value and am worthy of love"?
- In the simplest of terms, do I derive my love of self from God and God alone?

I know these are tough questions. Just saying "self-love" or "self-compassion" or "self-care" makes me feel selfish, because somewhere on my faith journey, faulty thinking—or cognitive distortion, as it is formally called—planted itself in my mind. When we understand the true meaning of being a selfish person, everything becomes much clearer. To be selfish is to be "concerned excessively or exclusively with oneself: seeking or concentrating on one's own advantage, pleasure, or well-being without regard for others."[50] Synonyms include egocentric, self-centered, self-absorbed, self-obsessed.

There we have it. Jesus's second greatest command doesn't instruct us to be self-centered, but God-centered (Mark 12:30)— because agape love for self and others flows out of a relationship with God. If that is out of sync, everything is out of sync. If I don't [agape] love God with all of my heart, soul, mind, and strength, I can't [agape] love myself, and ultimately, I can't [agape] love anyone else. When I have a God-centered love of self, it means I put on that oxygen mask first. I welcome God into my world and my whys because a threefold cord isn't easily broken (Practice 1). I live my life from my Genesis 2:7 beginning, my God-breathed place that fills me with an endless and eternal capacity and potential to love others well and deeply (Practice 2). That God-sized breath is full of the how-to's and the how-not-to's of making Mark 12:28–31 a very big reality in day-to-day life.

Reconnecting with Me, Myself, and I

I recently spent ten whole days in the Outer Banks of North Carolina, one of my favorite places on earth. After all these years, my husband and I have created quite a ritual. We drive far down Highway 12 to the more desolate areas of the coast, to the tri-villages of Waves, Rodanthe, and Salvo. This area is steeped in history and known for its exceptional water access—both sound and ocean are close to one another. People from all over the world go there to kiteboard and windsurf, but my husband and I go to experience the solitude. With rare public beach access, enjoying this refuge means walking farther and climbing over high, often very hot, sand dunes. It's not an exercise for the faint of heart. The reward? A long, wide stretch of uninhabited beach, typically laden with a treasure trove of unique shells and driftwood.

We shed our shoes, feel the sand beneath our feet, drop everything, look at each other, smile, and breathe it all in. With a certain degree of ceremony, Rob grabs the white pole of our beach umbrella and, with a few well-rehearsed, rhythmic, back-and-forth motions, plunges it deep into the sand. We have claimed this spot, like adventurous trekkers, as ours for the entire day.

There, hunkered under the safe refuge of my beloved beach

umbrella, I determine to reconnect with God and reclaim a great deal of strength. I place my brand-new beach hat with its SPF 50 protection on my head, draw my oversized canvas beach bag close, and dig deep to find my favorite book, *Gift from the Sea*, nestled inside a plastic bag—my prized possession, protected from the elements of wind and waves. I open it, hold it in my hands, and close my eyes. *Life doesn't get any better than right now. The ocean air. The sound of swirling waves and singing gulls. The brown pelican's precise in-flight choreography overhead.*

Sometimes Shedding Comes before Collecting

By far, one of the greatest lessons learned under my beach umbrella is that sometimes, shedding comes before collecting. "One learns first of all in beach living," writes Anne Morrow Lindbergh, "the art of shedding. How little one can get along with, not how much. Physical shedding to begin with, which then mysteriously spreads into other fields. Clothes, first. Of course, one needs less in the sun. But one needs less anyway, one finds suddenly. One does not need a closet-full, only a small suitcase-full."[51]

Lindbergh's timeless words take my breath away. Two entirely different decades, yet we both deal with choosing simplification over complication. We seek to avoid amassing mounds of stuff—physical, emotional, and spiritual—things that are sincerely unnecessary and, if allowed, will weigh us down and keep us from living the meaningful, abundant life promised to each one of us (John 10:10). If I may, I'd like to stand on the shoulders of this great literary giant and expand her thoughts to include how we can actually practice this fine art of shedding, today.

Five Simple Ways to Shed[52]

The shedding of vanity. Maybe you don't live near the ocean and you struggle to relate with all this ocean talk. That's okay; I think we can all agree that no matter where we live, we all deal to some degree with the issue of vanity. It's easy to care too much about our appearance, status, achievements, and so on. But at the beach, it's okay to wear the same clothes for a few days in a row. Who cares? We can abstain from wearing jewelry or fixing fancy meals or obsessing about perfect houses. What's a little sand in the carpet?

The shedding of hypocrisy. Anne writes, "The most exhausting thing in life, I have discovered, is being insincere. That is why so much of social life is exhausting; one is wearing a mask. I have shed my mask."[53] As I walk down the beach, I notice everyone is wearing the same thing—bathing suits, shorts and a T-shirt, flip-flops. I couldn't tell a brain surgeon from a truck driver. How refreshing.

The shedding of anxiety. At the beach, everyone seems relaxed. No obsessing over tidying up. No one looking at their phones (maybe a rare few). Beach towels hang from porches. Showers are taken outside. Women wear little or no makeup.

The shedding of complication. Who doesn't love a few days where the biggest question is, Will we take Doritos or SunChips to the beach? We forget about bills and politics and wars and responsibility. We let go and remember how to laugh, play games, float on a tube, and build sandcastles.

The shedding of the trifles and trappings of life. We get so caught up, don't we? We forget that the little things in life really are the big things. As an amateur conchologist (shell collector), my passion for one particular shell, the beautiful moon shell, has come to symbolize simplicity and serenity. The first time I ever picked one up, I placed it in the palm of my hand and snapped a photo. Months later, I came across this passage of Scripture, written by the wise King Solomon, "Better one handful with tranquillity than two handfuls with toil and chasing after the wind" (Ecclesiastes 4:6). Today, the moon shell sits on my desk as a daily reminder that life is meant to be savored and that amassing more is not always better.

HEART CARE

Reflect

Here in Practice 5, we will explore the sacred art of lectio divina. In simple terms, lectio divina is "the practice of being present to each moment in a heart-centered way. When we read and pray lectio, we see sacred text as God's living words being spoken to our hearts in the moment. The practice allows us to encounter God in an active and intimate way."[54] As you read the following portion of Scripture, place yourself in the moment. In the scene. What if you were actually there, transported through time? Engage your senses. What stands out to you? A specific line? The setting? A specific word? An action?

Psalm 23 is rich in visual imagery. As you read it aloud, as presented here from the Living Bible, walk into the words. Let the visual imagery awaken your imagination.

Because the Lord is my Shepherd, I have everything I need! He lets me rest in the meadow grass and leads me beside the quiet streams. He gives me new strength. He helps me do what honors him the most.

Even when walking through the dark valley of death, I will not be afraid, for you are close beside me, guarding, guiding all the way. You provide delicious food for me in the presence of my enemies. You have welcomed me as your guest; blessings overflow!

Your goodness and unfailing kindness shall be with me all of my life, and afterwards I will live with you forever in your home.

Reframe

In our hyper connected, supersonic speed-of-life existence, we are rarely quiet. But we are responsible for the health of our souls, and a healthy soul knows the power of silence. You've been working so hard; I know that. Take some time to rest now—to collect your strength. Budgets, circumstances, and seasons in life might not allow us to adventure to an island, but we can find our very own little islands of collecting strength, right in our communities. Dig deep, get creative, and you will find ways that are absolutely free. Yes, write yourself a permission slip. Here are some guiding questions:

- What brings a smile to your face? Gives your heart joy? Makes you happy? The sky is the limit here; nothing is too small, too big, or too silly.
- What is available to you? Doesn't cost a fortune? Sometimes the public library is a great place to find out about fun, free activities.
- Are there community events that offer opportunities to collect strength?

Reauthor

Hannah's praying and staying power led me to develop a concept I now call "resilient rest" or, as a good friend coined, "restilience." *Restilience* is a God-given endowment and enlargement of physical, emotional, and spiritual capacity to face personal, family, church, and work struggles from a sacred place of collected strength. By praying and staying with her pain, Hannah collected strength from God, stored it in the reservoir of her soul, and ultimately, as we read at the end of her story, received the fulfillment of her heart-wrenching journey—her beloved son, Samuel (1 Samuel 1:20).

A woman's greatest gift to everyone in her sphere of influence is emotional health and well-being. Consider the threefold cord of resilience training. The result: restilience.

Spiritual	Simple daily practices where we collect strength. This leads to a heart of rest. A heart at rest is a heart at its best.
Mental	Daily, minute-by-minute choices to transform emotion-driven behaviors—emotional regulation. Emotions are God-given, yet we are not to be ruled by them. Here, we pray for the fruit of the Spirit, especially self-control, to develop in our lives. Eventually, spiritual maturity unfolds like a beautiful, fragrant rose.
Physical	Continued, strategic, intentional development of the nine practices presented in this book.

Wait for the Peace that Passes All Understanding

The Intention of Practice 6:
I will overcome hurtful words by waiting
for the peace that passes all understanding.

While a crisis is a summons into transformation,
we must also recognize that it's an advent into an entanglement
of feelings. Part of living a crisis creatively is identifying
and understanding the feelings that come with it.
Otherwise, we don't have a crisis; it has us.
—SUE MONK KIDD[55]

When a heart breaks, it seems to scream for answers. Once the shock settles, it begs for a quick fix and instant healing. It runs to anyone who will listen; seeks relief from the anguish. The last thing on earth a broken heart wants is to sit down in the waiting room of life. No, it wants relief, and it wants it fast. Waiting rooms are not fashioned for the fainthearted or the impatient. You've been there, I'm sure. Sitting in a crowded room, waiting for a doctor's appointment or a loved one to come through surgery. Fingers tap on the armrests of chairs. Restless legs bounce up and down with nervous energy. Surrounded by strangers, stacks of magazines, and cups of instant coffee, heart rates increase as heightened emotions and anxious questions seem to tick . . . tick . . . tick . . . in sync with the clock on the wall. *How much longer do I have to wait? When will the doctor come and tell me what is going on? It's been hours. If something doesn't happen soon, I'm going to crawl out of my skin.*

It's true, waiting isn't something we typically welcome. Over the past five years, I stopped counting how many waiting rooms I've found myself in. I affectionately call this season my "passing through the valley of the shadow of waiting rooms." Between the medical crises of my daughter, my mother, and myself, life has been defined by sitting and waiting. These spaces stretch us in unimaginable ways and push us to the edge of our comfort zones, asking us to practice patience, something none of us are fond of these days.

One particular late-night-into-early-morning trauma with my mother found me in yet another waiting room, this time in a hospital surgical ward. With *The Price Is Right* blaring in the background, I tried to calm myself down. I read through several devotionals, including my favorite, *Streams in the Desert*, by L. B. Cowman. Her timeless words always reach deep into my soul. Her message on December 10 didn't disappoint.

Cartons containing spices from the Orient may be cumbersome to ship and slow in coming, but once they arrive, the beautiful fragrances fill the air. In the same way, suffering is trying and difficult to bear, but hiding just below its surface is discipline, knowledge, and limitless possibilities. Each of these not only strengthens and matures us but also equips us to help others. So do not worry or clench your teeth, simply waiting with stubborn determination for the suffering to pass. Instead, be determined to get everything you can from it, both for yourself and for the sake of those around you, according to the will of God.[56]

After reading her thoughts, I sent them to my daughter, Candace, a travel writer living abroad at the time. It wasn't long before the phone rang.

"Hey, Mom!"

"Candace? What on earth are you doing awake? It's three thirty a.m. where you are." I laugh, knowing she is the family night owl—a nocturnal being who does her best work in the wee hours of the morning.

"So, you're back in the waiting room?" she asked.

"Ah! Yes. Don't want to be here," I answer.

"I'm sure. It's like you've sold the house, moved out, and locked the door behind you. But now, you're having to move back again."

"True." I laugh again. "But I will say, this time I am not anxious or frustrated. That crawling-out-of-my-skin feeling has found its way to a place of rest."

For the next fifteen or twenty minutes, we had the richest conversation. I was digging for my pen and paper because the thoughts were flowing.

"How are you having these thoughts at six thirty a.m., Mom? Seriously?"

"How are you having these thoughts at three thirty a.m., Daughter? Seriously?"

Once again, the magic of the waiting room unleashed its power. Despite the zany characters hooting and hollering in the background on *The Price Is Right*, time slowed long enough for great thinking to make its way to the forefront of our minds and conversation.

I savor that conversation like a steamy cup of my favorite Kenyan tea.

Leaning into a Slower Pace

In the waiting room, life slows down, and in a strange way, we finally slow down. As time passes, if we cooperate and lean into practicing patience, something magical can happen. Previously important schedules are interrupted by the eternal. Things that earlier in the day seemed critical lose their sense of immediacy. Oftentimes, friends and family either call or appear with emotional support and much-needed reinforcements. Personal agendas are exchanged for God's agenda. Anxiety lifts and gives way to acceptance—the gateway to God's peace.

Healing Happens in Layers

You are halfway through this heartlifting journey. How are you doing so far? Your heart care has offered some challenges, but you have also found a safe place to be; your heart has returned to its Creator, learned the secret of collecting strength, and is ready to take the next step. Here in Practice 6, things are going to get a little more personal. As my own counselor told me, "Healing happens in layers. The deeper we go, the more personal it gets. But God is a gentleman; He doesn't push us around. He waits until we are ready to go deeper.

And then He goes with us. There is nothing more important to God than having an intimate relationship with you."

"Intimate?" I winced at her words. "God wants to be intimate with me? That sounds a bit strange."

"That is because you have a misconstrued idea of real intimacy. When I say 'intimate,' I am describing a very close friend. Someone you feel safe around. Someone who loves you for you. Think of it another way. Intimacy is sometimes explained, 'in-to-me-see.'" She smiled.

She was so right. I had no idea what a true intimate relationship was really all about. Together, we read two special verses about intimacy that helped so much. In John 15:9–10 (MSG), Jesus tells His followers, "I've loved you the way my Father has loved me. Make yourselves at home in my love. If you keep my commands, you'll remain intimately at home in my love. That's what I've done—kept my Father's commands and made myself at home in his love."

"'Intimately at home in my love,'" I repeated. "I'm definitely going to think long and hard about what that looks like in my life."

I started to read more about the subject of intimacy. One of the best explanations I found said it this way:

Real intimacy makes us feel alive like we've been found, as if someone finally took the time to peer into the depths of our soul and really see us there. Until then, until we experience true intimacy, we feel passed over and ignored, like someone is looking right through us. Real intimacy can only begin once you know yourself . . . true intimacy begins with being connected to your own heart. Because God made us, He intimately knows us better than anyone can.

He can make us feel known in a way that no one on earth is able.[57]

Being connected to our heart takes a great deal of time, self-compassion, and energy—as we're finding out. It also means we must spend time with the One who created our heart. Just the thought of this can sound daunting at first. Many of us see God as a regal king, sitting on an ornate throne. And this is true—He is a King. In Revelation 4, John, one of Jesus's closest followers, while exiled on the island of Patmos, was swept into an incredible vision of heaven. He wrote, "At once I was in the Spirit, and there before me was a throne in heaven with someone sitting on it. And the one who sat there had the appearance of jasper and ruby. A rainbow that shone like an emerald encircled the throne" (Revelation 4:2–3).

But the beauty of God is that He also became a man who walked on this earth (Philippians 2:6–7), taking on the very nature of a servant. He actually experienced, firsthand, every emotion and temptation known to us. Hebrews 2:18 (TLB) tells us, "Since he himself has now been through suffering and temptation, he knows what it is like when we suffer and are tempted, and he is wonderfully able to help us." And He does. He never expects us to walk this journey alone—even though, at times, it feels as if we are. He helps us *by His Spirit*, whom He promised to each one of us. I am certain of one thing: God never breaks His promises. Right before His death and resurrection, Jesus assured His followers, "I will ask the Father, and he will give you another advocate to help you and be with you forever—the Spirit of truth. The world cannot accept him, because it neither sees him nor knows him. But you know him, for he lives with you and will be in you. I will not leave you as orphans; I will come to you" (John 14:16–18).

This mystery is beautiful and baffling all at the same time, so I understand your need to just sit and take it all in. At this point on our journey, that is exactly what we are going to do.

When Your Heart Sits in God's Waiting Room

If you would, imagine with me for a minute, maybe two. Schedule some time for this meditative exercise. When everything calms down for the day or maybe on your lunch break, find somewhere quiet and let these words wash over you like rain. Read this narrative aloud, slowly and certainly.

Open your hand. Left or right; either works. Feel me place a golden key in your palm. My hand is resting on yours. Etched deeply in the center of the key is one word: 'owr.

"'O-w-r," you spell carefully, a bit unsure about this mysterious word. As you turn it over in your palm, you conclude, "This must be written in a foreign language."

"You are right," I explain. "It is a Hebrew word. Simply pronounced, ore, like the beautiful rock filled with vital minerals and elements."

For now, all I ask is that you trust me. Keep your special key close to your heart. You will need it soon.

See yourself standing in a narrow, dark hallway, outside a beautiful door. The door can be any shape, size, color, material you like. The sky is the limit. There are no boundaries on the creativity of design here. Dream big. And the best part, that door can be anywhere in the world.

You are holding a brown leather satchel. Inside is your history of hurts, the one you worked so hard on in Practice

3. Before you go any further, put the satchel down. Leave it in this dark hallway. It can't go where you are going. There won't be any room or use for it anymore. You've carried it as far and as long as it will go. Say good-bye.

Gently, put your hand on the doorknob. Initially it feels cold to the touch. You hesitate out of fear of the unknown; you feel uncomfortable not knowing what is on the other side. You close your eyes, take a deep breath, and start turning the knob.

You find it locked.

"Oh, the key. I need the key," you remember, digging into your pocket. It's not there. Oh, wait, you are clenching it in your hand. Slowly, with intention, you place the key in the lock. The doorknob heats up. A warm sense of calm flows from your head to your toes. Suddenly, you feel something, a slight flutter in your stomach. It's been quite a while since you've felt such a sensation . . . and it feels really nice. What is this feeling?

Hope? Is it hope? Can it be? Is there something good on the other side of this door? Is it even possible?

As you push the door, a sliver of light bursts through and, before you know it, you are engulfed in brilliant light. It's no ordinary light. You stand still, soaking in the warmth. Bask in this light. As it seeps into your being, you feel it adding strength. You even begin to smile. Wait, is that a giggle? Go ahead, let it out. This is what it feels like to be home. Full of joy. Anticipation. Expectancy.

Thoughts come to mind. This feels like Lucy entering Narnia. Alice in Wonderland falling down the rabbit hole. Dorothy opening her eyes in Munchkin Land. You sense that something equally as stunning and surprising and sincerely remarkable is waiting for you on the other side of that door.

"Go ahead," I urge with a gentle push. "Open the door. Step over the threshold."

"Aren't you coming with me?" you ask.

"No, not here. You have to go into this room alone. But I'll be close by."

You hear five words, lyrically spoken, "Welcome to your waiting room." The voice is familiar—warm and inviting, like the room.

"God?" you ask.

"Yes, it is me," He answers. "Welcome."

God invites you and your tender heart to come in and sit for a while. He's designed this space especially for you. No one else has a waiting room like yours.

What do you see? What does it look like? What color is the furniture? How is it decorated? What smells are swirling in the air? Is it inside or outside? Near the ocean or by a pristine lake? High on a mountaintop or nestled in a verdant valley?

Here, in this very special—dare I say, sacred—space, your heart is going to learn the language of love.

God invites you to sit down and asks to see your key. He brushes His finger over the etched word, as if He is admiring His very own handiwork.

"'Owr," God explains, "in Hebrew means 'light.' But 'owr is no ordinary light. It is the special light of illumination.

On the first day, in those first moments of creation, I spoke, 'Let there be light,' [Genesis 1:1]. 'Owr is that light. Light imbued with overcoming power.

"Here, in your waiting room, this same luminous power will shine into all the dark places in your heart, bringing the healing you are seeking. Light will break forth like the morning dawn. Healing will quickly arise. When our time here comes to an end, I promise you will leave full of the light of My love. People will call you a heartlifter— a woman filled with the light of My love. They will be drawn to you. Your radiant presence in their life will ease their heartrifting journey.

"Close your eyes, now. I have a surprise for you." God smiles. Then He puts something in your hand.

"Ah!" You smile back. "A brand-new satchel. Thank You!"

"Go ahead; open it," He says. "I know how much you loved your old satchel, so I wanted to give you this. Look inside."

As you open it, you see three envelopes inside.

"Go ahead. Take them out," God speaks softly.

The three envelopes have gilt edges and are tied together with the most beautiful twine. A little tag with the words "Especially for you" dangles off the twine. Crafted of the smoothest linen, you sense these letters are very special.

"My daughter," He says with love, "You have learned the power of a threefold cord. It is not easily broken. Each of these three envelopes holds special thoughts from My heart. Read them carefully. Take your time. That is why you are here, in this beautiful waiting room. Time has given you this gift. I'm here when you have any questions. I am always with you."

The room grows silent. You sit alone now, holding three special envelopes. You haven't felt this peaceful in quite some time. You don't want to leave; yet, you must.

It is time to cross the threshold into your God-breathed purpose and plan. The one only you can fulfill. Go, shine like the stars in the universe.

Let the Healing Begin

Since the beginning of time, God has placed the people He loves in unique and specific waiting rooms. Today, you find yourself in one. We often misunderstand these times of enforced rest, divine delay, or sudden sidelining as some form of punishment or neglect, when truthfully, God is drawing His child—and today, that is you—close to His heart. This calling aside for a season may be to further prepare you for a special purpose or perhaps to show you something you wouldn't see when rushing from here to there. Maybe it is just to remind you of how valuable you are to God. Every waiting room—past, present, and future—looks different, because each child is different. Consider these waiting rooms:

- Abram and Sarai pitched a tent in the middle of nowhere—waiting for their promise.
- Moses lived in a desert for forty years—waiting to set his people free.
- Joseph found himself in pits and prisons—waiting for his dream to come true.

- David dwelt in a pasture learning to care for sheep—waiting to become the king of Israel.
- Jonah ended up in the belly of a great fish—waiting to come to his senses.
- The eighty-four-year-old prophetess Anna sat in the temple—waiting to see the Promised One.
- John the Baptist ate locusts and honey in a wilderness—waiting to herald the Messiah.
- John lived out his days as a prisoner, exiled on the island of Patmos—waiting to hear what might be next for him and ultimately reveling in an extraordinary vision of a new heaven and a new earth.

As displeasing as the waiting process is, it is an essential part of our heartlift journey. We aren't privy to the private, inner struggles of the great men and women who have gone before us—the ancient text only gives us a brief peek into their lives—but we can guess they weren't thrilled with the waiting process either. Somewhere in the middle of it all, I imagine they found themselves yelling out to God like a small child in the backseat of the family car. "God, are we there yet? How much longer is this going to take? How much farther do we have to go? I want to get out of here!" At the end of their lives, as they were looking over their shoulders, did they see their time in the waiting room as worth it? I can only imagine they would all say, "Yes!"

Our heavenly Father's timing is exact. He sees the big picture, while we see only the now. Why does He make one person, like our dear Hannah, wait years, and another only a day or two? It is not for us to know. But there is great power inside the waiting room. Waiting and patience are intimate companions. One cannot exist without the other. Perhaps that is why our adversary, the author of all that is unhealthy and the father of lies, feeds the flame of our impatience.

Author Bob Sorge said it this way:

> Waiting on God is so powerful that the enemy will do everything in his power to dissuade you from maintaining your watch. He will tell you that you're insane to keep waiting on God in the midst of your pressing circumstances. He'll tell you that waiting on God is changing nothing. But there is a day coming when God will change everything in a moment of time. He may take seemingly forever to get around to it, but once God moves, He can change everything in a day.[58]

And that's even more reason to sit patiently in God's waiting room with an open heart and open hands—ready, willing, and able to receive.

To wait (or *qavah* in Hebrew) literally translates "to twist or bind like a rope, creating something stronger and more robust."[59] Might we say, like a threefold cord? The repetition of our narrative continues to strengthen, doesn't it?

- We are overcoming hurtful words together: the threefold cord of the heartlift journey involves you, me, and God.
- As we understand our God-breathed identity, we understand the threefold cord of connection: connection to God, to self, and to others.
- Rest empowers the threefold cord of me, myself, and I to move through life from a place of collected strength.

Twisting and binding don't really paint a comforting picture, do they? No, instead they imply momentary (depending on exactly how much time God sees fit to twist and bind) pain and discomfort—but ultimately, this action results in a strong, robust rope, and in our lives results in strong, robust, resilient character.

The Threefold Cord of Waiting

It is time to open our three letters. I don't know about you, but I am really excited to see what is inside. On the outside, each bears an inscription:

Letter One: *Turn your face toward the Light.*

Letter Two: *Let the Spirit of Truth be your guide.*

Letter Three: *Experience the Peace that passes all understanding.*

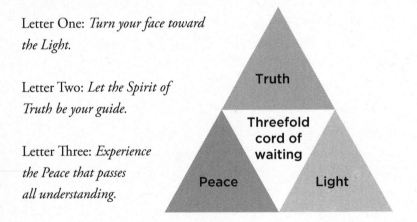

As you read through each letter, read them as if God is speaking to you—the only person in the entire world. It might be hard at first to adjust to this intimate narrative, but it becomes easier. Take your time, there is no rushing allowed in your waiting room. The longer we wait, the quieter it gets, the more intimate the questions become . . . leading us to the most significant question of all: "How do I want to live the rest of my life?

The Cord of Light:
Turn Your Face toward the Light

The world began with four powerful words, "Let there be light." I created light in the shape of a sun, the moon, and radiant stars (Genesis 1:14–16), and set them in the sky to illumine the earth. I then divided this light, creating a daytime and nighttime. I knew My creation needed both.

I know your need for light too. Hurtful words seem to turn the lights off, leaving you and your heartrift alone in the dark. Things look, sound, and feel different in the dark. Trees look like monsters. The wind sounds like a whistling intruder. Cold spaghetti feels like wriggling worms. A brief walk feels like a marathon. In the dark, the load seems like too much to bear. Your perspective changes. Your heart melts with fear and anxiety, and your surefootedness transforms into disorientation. Bottom line? Perspective needs to be realigned. I have a few thoughts on how to do this:

1. Turn your face toward the light. Become a light-oriented woman; live by the light-filled words written by My son, Matthew:

> Do not store up for yourselves treasures on earth, where moth and rust destroy, and where thieves break in and steal. But store up for yourselves treasures in heaven, where neither moth nor rust destroys, and where thieves do not break in or steal; for where your treasure is, there your heart will be also. The eye is the lamp of the body; so then if your eye is clear, your whole body will be full of light. But if your eye is bad,

your whole body will be full of darkness. If then the light that is in you is darkness, how great is the darkness! (Matthew 6:19–23 NASB)

2. I placed an internal clock within the young sunflower that causes it to face east at dawn to greet the sun. As the sun moves west throughout the day, the sunflower follows it. During the night, it slowly turns back to start the cycle again. As it matures, the overall growth slows down so the circadian clock makes sure the plant gets enough early-morning light for the whole day. I spent a great deal of time and energy on those six days of Creation, filling the natural world with life lessons, just for you.

3. Let the sunflower's beautiful story inform your new story. From this day forward, face east at dawn and greet My Son. Follow Him westward through the day, and then slowly turn back east to start again tomorrow. Be light-oriented. Fill your being with only those things that are light-producing. Follow hard after My son Paul's words in Ephesians 1:18 (TLB), "I pray that your hearts will be flooded with light so that you can see something of the future he has called you to share. I want you to realize that God has been made rich because we who are Christ's have been given to him!"

The Cord of Truth:
Let the Spirit of Truth Be Your Guide

Oh, how I want to keep your heart flooded with light. Healing words turn the lights back on. The light of my life-giving words leads you into all truth. Light and truth are intimates. Over and over again, we see them working together. My psalmist, a beloved son of Korah, sought their help in his daily life. Consider his prayer, "Oh, send out your light and your truth—let them lead me" (Psalm 43:3–4 TLB). He's asking for stability, surefootedness, and soundness. He longed to leave behind the lies that caused emotional instability in his life; he desired to live in the truth and light that brings emotional stability—being stable even when the forces of evil threaten instability.[60]

Listen closely, what I have to say to you now is very important. The only way you can change the negative, heartrifting narrative spoken over you is to

1. Turn to Me, your Counselor and Guide, and together, we will read the truth of My Word. A negative voice speaks: "You are not good enough." The truth speaks: "You made all the delicate, inner parts of my body and knit them together in my mother's womb. Thank you for making me so wonderfully complex! It is amazing to think about. Your workmanship is marvelous—and how well I know it" (Psalm 139:13–14 TLB).

   The brain handles positive and negative information in different hemispheres. Negative emotions generally involve more thinking, and the information is processed more thoroughly than positive ones. Thus, we tend to ruminate more about unpleasant events—and use stronger words to describe them—than happy ones.[61]

2. Turn to me, your heavenly Father, and think about how you talk to yourself. In your internal conversations—those intimate words you speak to your own heart, mind, soul, and body—be sure to speak more positive words than negative.

Literally turn down the volume on all the negative words, thoughts, or sentences. Tell them to be quiet. Identify a lie for what it is and reframe it with the truth. And always, be kind to yourself. Wake up and hear me say, "Good morning, daughter. When I created you, all of heaven smiled because you have immense value, worth, and dignity. I'm going to walk with you today. You will never be alone."

3. Turn your face east at dawn and invite Me, the Spirit of Truth, to walk with you through the day. When your feet hit the floor, greet the day with, "Good morning, Holy Spirit. Guide me into all truth today. Amen."

The Cord of Peace:
Experience the Peace that Passes All Understanding

Now, the final twisting on this threefold cord of waiting. As your heart is flooded with My light and believes My truth, peace comes. My peace is like nothing you have ever felt before. It is a peace that passes all understanding. At first, it might be hard to accept. Peace will feel strange. You've been distressed for so long. It will help to keep the words of my son Paul with you as you leave your waiting room:

Don't worry about anything; instead, pray about everything; tell God your needs, and don't forget to thank him for his answers. If you do this, you will experience God's peace, which is far more wonderful than the human mind can understand. His peace will keep your thoughts and your hearts quiet and at rest as you trust in Christ Jesus (Philippians 4:6–7 TLB).

What Really Matters

Time in the waiting room ultimately leads to the most important question of all: *How do I want to live the rest of my life?* Time in this very special place of waiting helps us see that we truly want to become heartlifters, not heartrifters. Before leaving, take time to add your voice to this prayer for unity:

> *Father God, help us be wise, not know-it-alls. May we be full of light, not empty and void. May we be accepting of one another, not rejecting. May we be authentic, not artificial. May we be kinder than we want to be, not catty and curt. May we be peacemakers, not peacekeepers. May we be joyful, not jealous. May we be truth-seekers, not tell-alls. May we be humble, not hateful or spiteful. May we be mature, not immature. And ultimately, Father, may we shine like the stars in the universe (Daniel 12:3), lighting up the skies of our spheres of influence. Amen.*

It will be hard to leave, but life must be lived. Tuck your three letters into your brand-new satchel, hold it close, and take one last deep breath before moving on. Now, go in peace. The best is yet to come.

HEART CARE

Reflect

Irish poet David Whyte in his beautiful poem "The Journey," speaks of "arriving." As you read through each word, what do his wise words speak to your heart?

Above the mountains
 the geese turn into
 the light again

Painting their
 black silhouettes
 on an open sky.

Sometimes everything
 has to be
 inscribed across
 the heavens

so you can find
 the one line
 already written
 inside you.

Sometimes it takes
 a great sky
 to find that

first, bright
    and indescribable
    wedge of freedom
    in your own heart.

Sometimes with
    the bones of the black
    sticks left when the fire
    has gone out

someone has written
    something new
    in the ashes of your life.

You are not leaving.
    Even as the light fades quickly now,
    you are arriving.[62]

Reframe:
Barriers to Intimacy with God

Barriers prevent forward movement and access to something. As you sat in your waiting room, what barriers or obstacles kept you from intimacy with Christ? Think about that as you read through James 4:8–10 (MSG):

So let God work his will in you. Yell a loud *no* to the Devil and watch him scamper. Say a quiet *yes* to God and he'll be there in no time. Quit dabbling in sin. Purify your inner life. Quit playing the field. Hit bottom, and cry your eyes out. The fun and games are over. Get serious, really serious. Get down on your knees before the Master; it's the only way you'll get on your feet.

What would saying a "quiet yes" to God look like in your life?

Reauthor

Oh, how I want you to have fun with this reauthoring. In your waiting room, God asked you what your waiting room would look like. Where would it be?

My vision? I want a tree house, preferably in Big Sur, that overlooks the Pacific Ocean. Can you see the whales breaching, the sea lions sunbathing? It's not an ordinary tree house; I'm asking big. Of course, it will face east, as I will need to wake every morning and turn my face that direction, toward the Light. . . . Ocean breezes fill the air with negative ions. Sunflowers grow twelve feet tall and can be seen from every window. There's no need for screens; there are no bugs. There is room for everyone I love to stay.

Your turn. Take as much time as you need to dream. The sky is the limit!

PART THREE: REAUTHOR

Future Freedom:
Will I Ever Trust Again?

Embrace a Teachable Spirit

The Intention of Practice 7:
I will overcome hurtful words
by embracing a teachable spirit.

Are you tired? Worn out? Burned out on religion? Come to me.
Get away with me and you'll recover your life.
I'll show you how to take a real rest. Walk with me and work
with me—watch how I do it. Learn the unforced rhythms of grace.
I won't lay anything heavy or ill-fitting on you.
Keep company with me and you'll learn to live freely and lightly.
—Matthew 11:29–30 MSG

Almost every day, I wear a beautiful necklace that bears the inscription *ancora imparo*, which translates, "I am always learning."[63] One morning while researching for an upcoming online college course I facilitate, I read something about the brilliant artist Michelangelo that caused me to pause. Well into his eighties, Michelangelo was heard saying, "I am still learning." Overwhelmed by his earnest humility, I sat back in my chair and thought long and hard about those four words, "I am still learning."

How on earth did this man, a true genius with such obvious artistic brilliance, feel like he had more to learn? I couldn't wrap my brain around such a thought. I've stood under Michelangelo's masterpiece, the ceiling of the Sistine Chapel in the Apostolic Palace, marveled at his seventeen-foot marble sculpture of *David* in Florence, and rested before the *Pietá* at St. Peter's Basilica (Vatican City), breathing in the agony of Mary holding her crucified Son. With all sincerity, I don't know what else this master could learn. His artistry reflects sheer perfection. Old age or not, here was a man deeply committed to learning more.

His thoughts became a driving force during this crushing season of my life. No matter how much we know or learn, there is still more. *If Michelangelo felt this way*, I thought, *shouldn't I?* What might happen if our world adopted this mind-set? If we set aside arrogance, pride, or bashing behaviors?

This Michelangelo mantra serves as a beautiful invitation to embrace a teachable spirit. I like to think I am teachable, but in case I get too big for my britches, I take the ceremonious time every morning to put those words around my neck, as if my day's productivity and success depend upon it. After I close the clasp of the necklace, I lay the palm of my hand over the words, repeat a quiet prayer, and start my day. This simple morning reminder serves as a gentle call to keep growing, as affirmed again in my favorite proverb, "Wise men and women are always learning, always listening for fresh insights" (Proverbs 18:15 MSG). Solomon and Michelangelo, two men at the top of their game, both agree we must keep learning and listening. True signs of a mature heart.

To Choose or Not to Choose

The heartlift process offers each of us a pivotal "to choose or not to choose" moment. We can choose a teachable spirit or choose to stay the same. We don't have to forgive. We don't have to heal. We don't have to do anything we don't want to do. That is the power of free will. Even as I write these thoughts, I hear whispers of Frankl's thought again—"between a stimulus and a response is a space."[64] That sacred space, as I call it, becomes a tipping point— "a critical moment in a complex situation in which a small influence or development produces a sudden large or irreversible change."[65] Life's multitude of hurtful moments leads to this one moment.

We find ourselves teetering, and we hesitate. *Do I hold on to the hate and anger I feel for this person who hurled hurtful words at me? Do I want to make the hard choice and forgive them? Do I want to dig deep and practice new healthy behaviors? If I do, I'll have to change. Not too sure it's worth my time or energy. No matter what I do, nothing changes anyway.*

I see the angst of this moment unfold every day. Whether in my office with a client, talking to women at retreats, or sitting across from someone at Starbucks, that moment of hesitation fills the air, and a choice has to be made. The air is so heavy I can feel it. Hesitation and uncertainty linger because unhealthy behavior patterns are as comfortable as an old pair of shoes. When hate is all you know, you choose hate. When dysfunction is all you know, you choose dysfunction. When guarding a grudge is all you know, you guard the grudge. So, with bated breath, I lean in, pray silently for courage, and wait. Eternity balances in that sacred space between hesitation and action.

Deborah knew all about the harmful effects of hesitancy. She came to me with a heavy heart.

"I'm so tired of hating her," she cried. "So tired."

"I know," I said. "I've been right where you are, and it is exhausting. How about we take care of your heart today and release this all into God's capable hands?"

"I just don't know." She cried even harder. "I want to let it go, but I've been holding this grudge in my heart for so many years, it will feel strange to live without it. I just don't know if I can."

It was Deborah's very own moment to choose or not to choose.

"Grudges are smudges on the face of our hearts," I shared, leaning in and taking Deborah's hands in mine. "Today is the day to get rid of this grudge and start living out the love. I'm here to help you. Let me give your grudge a little nudge. What do you say?"

Deborah took a deep breath, bowed her head, and nodded yes. Together, we prayed.

Deborah had a choice.

You have a choice.

Let Love In; Let Love Win

What choice will you make in that moment? The question begs an answer. I urge you, like Paul urged those following behind him, to choose the remarkable love and life God has for you. Let love in. Let love win. This is so important that I ask you to pause for a moment. Let's pray these powerful words together. Oh, how I wish we were face-to-face. We aren't, but we can be heart-to-heart. The psalmist tells us that God sends forth His word and heals (Psalm 107:20), so I take this as encouragement and send these healing words to you from Ephesians 3:14–19 (TLB):

> When I think of the wisdom and scope of his plan, I fall down on my knees and pray to the Father of all the great family of God—some of them already in heaven and some

down here on earth—that out of his glorious, unlimited resources he will give you the mighty inner strengthening of
his Holy Spirit. And I pray that Christ will be more and
more at home in your hearts, living within you as you trust
in him. May your roots go down deep into the soil of God's
marvelous love; and may you be able to feel and understand,
as all God's children should, how long, how wide, how deep,
and how high his love really is; and to experience this love
for yourselves, though it is so great that you will never see
the end of it or fully know or understand it. And so at last
you will be filled up with God himself.

So often our hesitancy holds us back, and we stop shy of "being
filled up with God himself." Within these five verses in Ephesians,
Paul shows us five ways to press through this hesitancy and embrace
the teachable spirit that leads us to the true freedom in Christ we
desire.

1. A teachable spirit bows down in humility and surrender to
   God, as if to say, "God, I am so tired of living with these
   grudges, with this _____. Help me give up
   my grudges and live out the love in my life" (v. 14). It can
   also look like, "God, I don't want to be a know-it-all or a
   _____ anymore. Help me change." Fill in the
   blanks with your desire.
2. A teachable spirit prays first and acts second (v. 16), even if it
   is just a brave three-word prayer: "God help me."
3. A teachable spirit welcomes the mighty inner strengthening of
   the Holy Spirit (v. 16), and receives the power and courage to
   break through any barriers.

4. A teachable spirit trusts in God's plan over personal plans (vv. 14, 17), always giving God the space to verify, delay, or ultimately rewrite our plans.

5. A teachable spirit roots deep into the soil of God's marvelous love (vv. 18–19), committing to the ancora imparo way.

Rest in the embrace of this teachable spirit. There's no safer place to be. As hard as it is to trust God (and we will talk more about this in Practice 8), He can be trusted. To your tender heart, this seems almost impossible, but as you continually fall into the embrace of a good heavenly Father and begin relating to Him as your heavenly Father (spend time with Him and the words He left for you), intimacy takes your hand, wisdom guides you, and before you know it, you'll have moved through the pain.

Call me an optimist; I am. Call me childlike; I am. God's words on a page become active, living, breathing realities that are available to help. I take them at face value. Jesus made it very clear that we are to keep a childlike faith. His followers came to Him and wanted to know how they could be great in the kingdom of God. What did Jesus do? He pulled a child onto His lap and said, "I assure you and most solemnly say to you, unless you repent [that is, change your inner self—your old way of thinking, live changed lives] and become like children [trusting, humble, and forgiving], you will never enter the kingdom of heaven. Therefore, whoever humbles himself like this child is greatest in the kingdom of heaven" (Matthew 18:3–4 AMP).

Right in front of their eyes, Jesus's followers saw a picture of a teachable spirit—a child. The Amplified Bible interprets His words so clearly, encouraging us to develop malleable hearts that will commit to changing old ways of living. When we become like children, still unmarred by life's tough places, we can live out His words in changed lives.

You Were Created to Be Loved

On a very cold March afternoon, while on a writing-this-book break, I made my way to the newly released movie *The Shack*. Years earlier, I had read William P. Young's controversial book of the same title and was eagerly anticipating seeing the narrative on the big screen. Being a visual learner, movies speak loudest to me. Books are great, but if my eyes can see it, that's even better. I wasn't disappointed. I took four pages of notes—in the dark!

There on the big screen, my understanding of God the Father, or as He's called in the movie, "Papa," grew. When I first read the book, I couldn't process calling God "Papa." It almost made me cringe. But it's been ten years since I read it for the first time, and the deep, inner healing and reauthoring of my personal heartlifting journey has brought me to the place where calling God by this intimate, endearing name seems perfectly natural.

Several *aha* moments happened as I watched, but one toward the end of the movie did me in. Mackenzie, the father whose daughter was abducted, is taken back to the scene of the crime. He turns to God and asks, "Why did You bring me back to the place of my deepest pain?"

God looks right at him. "Because this is where you got stuck. When all you see is your pain, you lose sight of Me."

Pick me up off the sticky theater floor. I lost it. Being right in the middle of writing this book, I thought, *Yes! There it is!* I couldn't write fast enough.

The God character continues, "You, on the other hand, were created to be loved. Living unloved is like clipping a bird's wings. Pain has a way of doing that to us. If it's left unresolved, you can forget what you were created for. That's not something I want for you. That's why you are here, Mackenzie. This is your flying lesson."

Later, the Holy Spirit adds to this conversation, showing Mack a crystal vial.

"What is that?" Mack asks.

With grace and tender empathy, the Spirit looks at Mack. "We all collect things we value. I collect tears."

As the movie closes, the Holy Spirit uses the vial of tears to water the grave of Mack's little girl. Immediately, and quite magically, a tree grows and blossoms.

As the closing credits rolled, I sat in that dark movie theater thinking of you. Yes, you. When God told Mack that pain has a way of making us forget why we were created, I had already written the words of Practice 3 and your Genesis 2:7 beginning. I felt both affirmed and excited at the same time.

"Yes, God," I prayed. "May every person who picks up *Overcoming Hurtful Words* remember why they were created, too. Amen."

Let Pain Tutor You

God loves you so much that He can't bear to see you stuck in your pain. Romans 2:4 (MSG) says, "God is kind, but he's not soft. In kindness he takes us firmly by the hand and leads us into a radical life-change." He simply waits for us to ask. His Father heart hopes, like any good parent, that we will finally get tired of fighting against the pain and harboring the hurt and that we will come to Him.

The wisest piece of advice I've ever read I found in the helpful book *Strong Women, Soft Hearts* by author and counselor Paula Rinehart. These words have affected me greatly:

> It is easy to build small lives around the pain we encounter, to get lost in one thread of the plot of the story and miss the big theme. We can, unfortunately, build a monument to our woundedness. We can shape an identity around the things we've suffered. But somewhere in this, our hearts become frozen in place, and the real life God has given becomes hidden, even to us. If you want to know real joy in your life, then be willing to let pain tutor you.[66]

Inside her waiting room, Hannah let pain tutor her. We did the same, didn't we? As we sat with God, patient and still, we resisted the urge to become callous and instead opened our hearts. Tender to the touch, but risking it all on the chance to learn more about God, ourselves, and loving others deeply.

Medical intuitive and author of *Why People Don't Heal and How They Can*, Dr. Caroline Myss writes,

> We are not meant to stay wounded. We are supposed to move through our tragedies and challenges and to help each other move through the many painful episodes of our lives. By remaining stuck in the power of our wounds, we block our transformation. We overlook the greater gifts inherent in our wounds—the strength to overcome them and the lessons we are meant to receive through them. Wounds are the means through which we enter the hearts of other

people. They are meant to teach us to become compassionate and wise.[67]

The Greater Gifts Inherent in Our Wounds

When Hannah left her God-designed waiting room, she was different. Hannah's story didn't end with the birth of Samuel. She went on to bear seven more children and live a long, meaningful life. No clues are given about the relationship she and Penni had later in life, but one thing is certain—Hannah was different.

Like Hannah, we each set aside our satchels filled with our history of hurts, entered the waiting room, and spent time with God in that intimate place where we connected to how we wanted to live the rest of our lives. We left different, too—healthy women committed to gaining valuable interpersonal relationship skills so no future heartrifts can keep us from living our remarkable, God-breathed lives.

Learning the Language of Love

The language of love is layered with learning the tension between tough and tender. Love is both. The situation with Angela opened my eyes and invited me to learn a whole new, almost foreign, language of love. My family of origin—the family I grew up in—modeled dysfunctional modes of behavior patterns and communication skills. It was not all bad; I had loving parents and siblings, but when an alcoholic father is at (or often missing from) the helm, the family system suffers. As I learned this new language of love, I learned what healthy interpersonal relationships really look like. This was grueling, I must admit, because changing cognition—the way we think and act about something—is like starting all over.

As I learned more about the tensions of love—that sometimes it is tough and sometimes it is tender—I learned some techniques for building and maintaining good relationships.

- *Forgive but do not forget (Colossians 3:13).* A wise man once told me that forgiveness doesn't erase the pain, it releases us from the control of the one who hurt us and helps us remember the essence of the pain—which I lovingly call "an emotional scar." A tender place—healed, yet serves to remind of the work done in our hearts. In remembering the essence, we have an enlarged capacity to practice empathy with others and a spiritual resilience that fortifies. Moving forward, we live out the Golden Rule with greater passion—loving others as we want to be loved (Matthew 7:7–12). I liken this to a physical scar

- *Speak the truth in love (Ephesians 4:14–15).* So often, this passage is misinterpreted and miscommunicated. Paul is not telling the Ephesians they can say whatever they want to whomever they want as long as it is done "in love." Two important things are rarely spoken of in light of speaking the truth in love: First, Ephesians 4:14 shows that Paul is talking about speaking the truth in love about the gospel of Jesus, warning His followers to not "be tossed to and fro" by false teaching. Second, the conjunctive adverb "instead" is rarely mentioned, though it joins these two verses. Read one without the other, and we have a big misunderstanding. Moving forward, we understand we *don't* have permission to say whatever we want to whomever we want.

- *Act with discretion (James 1:19–20).* Discretion is "the

quality of behaving or speaking in such a way as to avoid causing offense or revealing private information."[68] Can you hear the mic drop here? How often is "I have a prayer request" a camouflage for gossip or unnecessary sharing among our fellow believers? I'm thinking that pretty soon, psychologists will develop yet another new malady in our counseling verbiage: Discretion Deficit Syndrome. Our world has lost any and all sense of discretion and desperately needs it back. James 1:19–20 (AMP) should be tattooed on our hearts:

> Understand this, my beloved brothers and sisters. Let everyone be quick to hear [be a careful, thoughtful listener], slow to speak [a speaker of carefully chosen words and], slow to anger [patient, reflective, forgiving]; for the [resentful, deepseated] anger of man does not produce the righteousness of God [that standard of behavior which He requires from us].

Moving forward, we will live out Psalm 141:3 (AMP), "Set a guard, O LORD, over my mouth; keep watch over the door of my lips [to keep me from speaking thoughtlessly]."

- *Reauthor limiting beliefs (Hebrews 12:2).* Every person in the world lives by a set of internal beliefs. Some constrain. Some are oppressive in nature. Some are absorbed in our childhood, as we've talked about. Some are learned. Some are the result of hurtful words. All can be reauthored. How can I be so sure? Because Hebrews 12:2 (AMP) reminds us that God is both Author and Finisher. He helps us transform negative narratives into beautiful new narratives—filled with healing and hope. However or wherever we've taken these limiting beliefs on, it is time for them to go. Bruce Frankel, author of *What Should I Do with the Rest of My Life?* writes, "The keys to overcoming many of these are recognizing them, understanding how we got them, and then banishing them through sustained activity."[69] The fact that you are holding this book in your hands shows your desire to overcome. I couldn't be prouder of you. As you put into practice the words written here, success is on its way. Moving forward, we will reauthor our limiting beliefs with the powerful words God says about us. We are enough. We are loved. We are valuable. The list goes on.

- *Establish healthy boundaries and accountability (Galatians 5:1).* Volumes have been written on the subject of boundaries, yet I still struggle with setting them. Maybe you know how I feel. My inability is directly tied to my misunderstanding of selfless vs. selfish. It is also a limiting belief: I can't say no. In 1992, Drs. Cloud and Townsend wrote their first book, *Boundaries.* Little did they know the impact their words would have. They have become go-to experts on setting boundaries, helping millions take control of their lives again (visit: www. boundariesbooks.com). Take any time you need to revisit our conversation about this in Practice 4. Moving forward, we will live in the freedom of Christ, as expressed in Galatians 5:1 (MSG), "Christ has set us free to live a free life. So take your stand! Never again let anyone put a harness of slavery on you." You can think for yourself! Trust your own voice. When in doubt? Let Proverbs 13:20 (MSG) be your guide: "Become wise by walking with the wise; hang out with fools and watch your life fall to pieces."

- **End the relationship (Luke 6:43–45).** No matter how hard you try, sometimes the only option is to end or leave the relationship. As I became healthy and understood what healthy love looked like, I understood this. It was hard to do, as I felt I should be able to make those relationships work. Surround yourself with healthy people—not perfect people, but people committed to being healthy. If you need help discerning this, I strongly advise you to seek help. Jesus clearly noted in Luke 6:43–45 that we can tell if a person is healthy by looking and examining their "fruit." Moving forward, we will remember that we have permission to end a relationship that is consistently unhealthy. Seek help from professionals or wise men and women who can walk you through this process.

- **Practice assertiveness (Matthew 5:33–37).** Tucked in the middle of the famed Sermon on the Mount, Jesus shares a message about oaths, in which He instructs His followers to be assertive and decisive. Not wishy-washy or tickling ears. One section, Matthew 5:33–37, packs quite the punch. In *The Message*, author and pastor Eugene Peterson interprets Jesus's words in a way we can really understand. He titles these verses "Empty Promises," and writes:

  > Don't say anything you don't mean. This counsel is embedded deep in our traditions. You only make things worse when you lay down a smoke screen of pious talk, saying, "I'll pray for you," and never doing it, or saying, "God be with you," and not meaning it. You don't make your words true by embellishing them with religious lace. In making

your speech sound more religious, it becomes less true. Just say "yes" and "no." When you manipulate words to get your own way, you go wrong.

Moving forward, it's simple: say what you mean and mean what you say. My friend Sarah taught me this. Early on in our friendship, I didn't want to hurt her feelings or say no to anything. So I sometimes agreed to things but then canceled or made up a silly excuse as to why I couldn't commit. She eventually saw through this smoke screen and called me on it.

"Let your yes be yes and your no be no," she said. "Make up your mind."

Life is all about people. There is no doubt, then, that we will face challenging relationships and be asked to put our brand-new WHOLE power tool into practice. We will welcome God into our whys, hold on in order to respond not react, overcome unhealthy with healthy, lean in and listen between the lines, and always do our best to elevate the atmosphere. I don't know about you, but I feel smarter and kinder and better already. That is the beautiful fruit of embracing a teachable spirit. We grow. We live into our very best selves.

HEART CARE

Reflect

Get comfortable and settle in. Read through Ephesians 3:14–19, in lectio divina fashion, reading in a slow, contemplative manner. Place yourself in these verses, so vibrant with visual imagery. As you read, listen for the whisper that speaks, *Take notice of this word. This phrase. This image.* What is God saying to you? I usually sense a word, and it causes my mind to pause. As you read, move through the three steps of lectio divina: meditation, contemplation, and prayer.

Reframe

There can be great challenges when learning a new language. Here, in Practice 7, we addressed some behavior patterns that might need to be reframed in our lives. We looked into how we forgive but do not forget, speak the truth in love, act with discretion, reauthor limiting beliefs, establish healthy boundaries and accountability, end the relationship, and practice assertiveness. Which of these behavior patterns gives you the greatest challenge? Never hesitate to seek professional help. Sometimes, we need a trained guide to help in these areas.

Reauthor

Perhaps one of Hannah's most beautiful lessons came when she understood the tension between tough love and tender care. I like to call this "The Lesson of Barren but Not Beaten." She was physically and emotionally barren, but in the midst of all of this barrenness, she thrived spiritually. Things looked bad on the outside, but inwardly, in that place that only God can see, Hannah was becoming a new woman: tough and tender all at the same time.

In what ways are you learning about these two sides of love? Tough and tender. I particularly love the "rough and careless handling" aspect of this definition. When we are "rough and carelessly handled" by those we trust, how do we stand firm and administer tough love? And how do we mingle tenderness inside of that? This delicate balance will take practice, but that is why we are here. Remember, you are not alone.

Tough[70]	Tender[71]
1. Able to withstand great strain without tearing or breaking; strong and resilient.	1. Easily crushed or bruised; considerate and protective; characterized by or expressing gentle emotions; loving.
Synonyms: durable, resilient, sturdy, rugged, solid, long-lasting, made to last.	**Synonyms:** caring, kind, tenderhearted, warmhearted, affectionate, softhearted, generous, giving, maternal.

Take the Leap and Trust Again

The Intention of Practice 8:
I will overcome hurtful words
by taking the leap and trusting again.

There is freedom waiting for you,
on the breezes of the sky, and you ask,
'What if I fall?' Oh, but my darling, what if you fly?[72]
—Erin Hanson

It was a rash decision, but one that held no regret. I was working out at my local gym when Scott, the owner, breezed by and shouted out a question.

"Janell, you've got to join us." He grinned. "You ready to take the leap?"

"Leap?" I asked. "What leap might that be?" Sweat dripped down my face.

"The gym is hosting a special group jump at the Suffolk Executive

Airport. It's time to experience that free fall you've been talking about. Are you ready?"

Scott and Bruce, co-owners of the gym, were both professional skydivers. We had been talking about a possible future jump so I could test some material I'd been developing. Never in a million years did I think it would ever pan out.

Truthfully, I surprised myself when, with no hesitation at all, I replied, "Yes! Absolutely!"

After my workout, I went home and told my husband, Rob.

"What? Are you serious?" he asked.

"Yep. Join me! It's on Father's Day. Perfect time to do it," I said. "All in the name of research."

"I don't know about this." It took a couple of days, but Rob did reluctantly decide to take the leap with me.

"On one condition," he said. "We jump at different times, just in case."

Ever the realist, I had to wisely agree. *Just in case.*

Claim the Courage

In her book *Strong Women, Soft Hearts*, author Paula Rinehart talks about living life courageously. She reminds us that God calls us to live boldly:

> It turns out that playing it safe, at least in matters of the heart, is the most dangerous thing you can do. By that route, you become a butterfly pinned to the wall, with wonderful colors and all kinds of potential but going nowhere. Your wings are clipped. To really fly you must claim the courage to live out of your real self, the one God called into being.[73]

For as long as I can remember, trusting in God seemed to go hand in hand with the proverbial leap of faith. With intense curiosity, I began my own search to see the parallels between trusting in God and taking a real leap of faith. My study started in a hotel room in Chicago with simple definitions, a Bible concordance, and Scripture reading. It continued through several years of deep valleys, dark places, and hours in waiting rooms. I had undertaken book projects, written many blog posts, and taught numerous conferences—all from speculation, not real-life experience.

So when Scott brought his skydiving idea to my attention, I decided it couldn't be a coincidence. Here was a prime opportunity to test my novice theory, to see if what I had been teaching was, in fact, true. I suspect that is why I didn't hesitate. Figuratively, I had already taken the jump in my mind a hundred times, so experiencing it firsthand seemed like the next logical step. No more guessing; it was time to put my words to the test.

My research proved 100 percent accurate. The tandem jump from fifteen thousand feet in the air definitely confirmed my notion—that taking a literal leap into the vast blue skies from a moving airplane is the perfect metaphor for trusting in God.

Thrust into the Depths of Trust

Trust. What a word. What a vast shadow this five-letter word casts. I found it a difficult concept to understand, and decided to do a little research. Bear with me, please, as we get to the core of the meaning and impact of trust. Time here is well spent, as trust is an essential principle of life. It is the foundation of so many things in our lives. Our faith. Our relationships. Our family bonds. Our governments. So much.

Webster, in his original 1828 dictionary, offers this definition of trust. Eager to be accurate, I've gone ahead and taken our study one step further, investigating the relatives of trust: reliance, veracity, and integrity, as they are closely linked and helpful in understanding trust more completely:

Trust (verb)[74]	Reliance (verb)[75]
1. A reliance or *resting of the mind* on the integrity, veracity, justice, friendship, or other sound principle of another person. 2. Firm belief in the reliability, truth, ability, or strength of someone or something.	*Rest or repose of mind*, resulting from a *full belief* of the veracity or integrity of a person, or the certainty of a fact.
Take notice: resting of the mind and "on the" portion of this definition. Trust has to be "in" or "on" someone or something.	**Take notice:** rest of mind and a full belief.

Veracity (noun)[76]	Integrity (noun)[77]
Habitual truth.	The quality of being honest and having strong moral principles; moral uprightness.

Veracity (noun)[76]	Integrity (noun)[77]
Synonyms: truthfulness, accuracy, correctness, faithfulness, fidelity, reputability, sincerity, honesty. Veracity is the cornerstone of God's character. Numbers 23:19 (esv) says, "God is not a man that he should lie, nor a son of man, that he should change his mind."	**Synonyms:** honesty, honor, good character, righteousness.

Once again, we look at the words within the words. They are so intricately woven together that one word is in the definition of the other:

- Trust and reliance go hand in hand. They are intimately acquainted. One can't work without the other. Genuine trust and reliance both require a full belief in the one being trusted. In our case, the One we are speaking of is God. Full belief must be active in order to truly trust in God. *Full* belief, not half-hearted, maybe-I'll-think-about-it trust.
- When we trust, we enjoy a "rest or repose of mind." Since we've defined *rest* as being the art of collecting strength in our souls, perhaps we can now interpret *trust* as collecting strength in our minds. When I first discovered how trust is

linked to the mind, I was shocked. *Of course it is. The greatest battles typically involve our thought processes and perceptions.*

- Following this path of reasoning, if trust brings rest to our minds, shouldn't it also bring peace to our hearts and health to our physical beings? Think of the ramifications: a reduction of anxiety and stress levels, increased overall wellness, and more productive sleep patterns—all proven to add meaning and satisfaction to life. The prophet Isaiah tried to tell God's people this: "People with their minds set on you [God], you keep completely whole, steady on their feet, because they keep at it and don't quit. Depend on GOD and keep at it because *in the LORD GOD* you have a sure thing" (Isaiah 26:3–4 MSG, emphasis mine). Why, oh why, don't we listen? Here it is. Another secret to living in the freedom we so desire.

Typically, we hear the word *trust* attached to the little preposition "in." We're to trust *in God.* Trust *in the Lord.* Put your trust *in me.* Trust *in our relationship.* Trust *in the leadership.*

But trust is elusive. We can't touch it; in fact, we almost have to experience it before we can define it. Yet we are to give it to some invisible reality, to God, or to some other entity. It's like trying to capture the wind, bottle the lily's fragrance, or catch a falling star. It requires a transaction in the spiritual realm of life, not the physical:

The intangible object → Our trust
The invisible reality → God

This is a high-stakes risk, would you agree?

Tandem Trust

When I said yes to my first skydive, my decision was based firmly on the fact that I would have a tandem guide. I would never have jumped out of that moving airplane without Jim, my guide, strapped to my back.

First and foremost, I trusted that Jim knew what he was doing and that he was well trained. He was trustworthy. I'd never met him before and didn't look at his credentials, but within an hour of meeting him, we jumped. I put my naïve trust—i.e., my full belief—in the airport, the skydiving company, and Jim.

Seriously—if I can put my trust in a complete stranger, why can't I put my trust in God?

This entire experience led me to a simple truth: before we take the leap and trust again, we must believe the person is trustworthy—that is, safe and dependable. The root of *dependable* (depend) points back to the idea of being "attached or fastened to."[78] Tandem guide Jim and I were definitely and thankfully very attached—and quite uncomfortably, I might add. We were fastened together by tightly constricting belts and buckles.

As my feet dangled over the edge of the plane's doorway, I saw nothing but blue skies and clouds before me. Until this point, I'd been as chill as a cucumber. All that changed in an instant. Sitting there, with the wind rushing and my heart racing, I thought, *I'm good. I don't need to go any further. Can we stop now?* Of course, Jim couldn't hear a word I was saying, but I'm guessing he could feel my body shaking. Sheer, utter panic swept over me. But there was no time left for that. Tandem Jim grabbed my forehead, pushed my head back into his chest, rocked three times . . . back, forth, back, forth, back, forth . . . and *boom!*

What happened next is a blur. All thought was gone—*poof.* Instead of a graceful, ballerina-like jump into the air, we tossed and tumbled like towels in the dryer. Complete and utter disorientation. And in that moment, one thought rolled with me: *I am going to die. I am going to die. I am going to die.*

For the entire extent of the free fall—approximately forty-five to ninety seconds at 120 mph, that was all I thought about. Mentally, I said good-bye to my husband, my kids . . . my mother and sister, waiting on the ground. I couldn't breathe; I sincerely thought I might be having a heart attack. The air was freezing cold. The physical toll actually made me forget that a parachute was involved. I was sure I was heading straight to the ground to die.

Seeking *the Answer*, Not the *answers*

Time and time again, difficult relationships and the hurtful words that walk into the room with them thrust us into the vast unknown of uncharted, accelerated emotions. Sheer panic sends us into faulty thinking. Emotional regulation flies out the window. We've talked all about these things. Now, your heart dangles over the precipice of trusting again. Opening your heart to trust is the ultimate spiritual and emotional free fall. I know for a fact that they feel the same. When that moment comes—and it will—you will face this looming question: *Do I believe God is trustworthy?* You'll soon find, however, that the question leads to a deeper, underlying question: *Who is God to me?*

A. W. Tozer's classic, *The Knowledge of the Holy*, begins with a profound statement: "What comes into our minds when we think about God is the most important thing about us."[79]

We have to stop and ask why. Why is what we think about God the "most important thing about us"? Tozer continues:

The history of mankind will probably show that no people has ever risen above its religion, and man's spiritual history will positively demonstrate that no religion has ever been greater than its idea of God. Worship is pure or base as the worshiper entertains high or low thoughts of God. For this reason the gravest question before the Church is always God Himself, and the most portentous fact about any man is not what he at a given time may say or do, but what he in his deep heart conceives God to be like. We tend by a secret law of the soul to move toward our mental image of God.[80]

Then, in plain and simple language, Tozer brings a brighter light.

Were we able to extract from any man a complete answer to the question, "What comes into your mind when you think about God?" we might predict with certainty the spiritual future of that man. Our real idea of God may lie buried under the rubbish of conventional religious notions and may require an intelligent and vigorous search before it is finally unearthed and exposed for what it is.[81]

Recently, due to my personal frustration and angst over an inability to help several of my clients heal their perception of God, I immersed myself in a quest to increase my own capacity to ask better questions. The standstill in their progress agitated me, in a good way, because it stretched my comfort zones. The answers, methods, and textbook knowledge I had was not helping. Having experienced the power of a perfectly timed, well-formulated, Spirit-filled question in my own healing work, I hungered to possess this skill. I studied the Socratic method, based on the wise Greek philosopher's capacity to foster critical thinking that draws out underlying belief systems. I walked through the Gospels with Jesus, examining His teaching style and the use of His discerning, well-timed questions. I scoured through magazine articles and online courses. These great teachers share one commonality: great questions lead students to dig deep within their hearts, where the deeper truths can be found. Every great teacher understands that it is far better for students to discover the truth themselves than to be told, as this leads to internalizing or owning the answer.

A whole new methodology opened up. With great intention, I began talking less, interrupting less, and as a result, started listening, not just hearing more. It was quite a feat for a loquacious woman. There is a huge difference between listening and hearing. Listening involves leaning in. We choose to listen. Hearing just happens. A car horn blows, and we hear it; we don't necessary listen to it. A client talks. I hear her, but I don't necessarily listen. I must lean in and actively listen between the lines to really hear what she is saying. This involves a great deal of intention, concentration, and processing.

As I changed, I began to notice a pattern with my clients. The deeper our heart work went, the fewer questions they asked. They became quieter, more pensive, and less anxious. They felt no need to fill the empty space with empty words.

In a session with a lovely young woman named Jill, she looked over at me and said, "Sometimes we have to seek the Answer, not the answers, right?"

These are two very different things. Seeking the *Answer* and not the *answers* leads to a place where surface answers aren't important anymore. Instead, the search leads us to peace that passes all understanding. To joy unspeakable and full of glory (1 Peter 1:8 KJV). Like Paul, we find something far more valuable than answers to our questions. In Philippians 3:7–8 (TLB), Paul wrote:

> All these things that I once thought very worthwhile—now I've thrown them all away so that I can put my trust and hope in Christ alone. Yes, everything else is worthless when compared with the priceless gain of knowing Christ Jesus my Lord. I have put aside all else, counting it worth less than nothing, in order that I can have Christ.

Now we know what Paul knew all those years ago. When hurtful words are spoken, we free fall. We're thrust into the unknown and it becomes quite disorienting. We run to anybody who will listen, or we close the blinds and hide. Sometimes we do both. We get mad at God for letting it happen. We do whatever we can to numb the pain.

Eventually we wear ourselves out and realize we've been putting our trust in everything but God. That's when we can finally settle down long enough to be quiet and listen. If we are willing and teachable, we will sit in God's waiting room, where the Holy Spirit will gently guide and help us put our hope and trust in God—the Answer. Suddenly, the answers don't really matter anymore, because we know the Answer, who in time will reveal exactly what we need to know.

Jill's well-timed, Spirit-filled question, "Sometimes we have to seek the Answer, not the answers, right?" ushered in a beautiful, healing moment. This heartshift led us to a beautiful meditative exercise in which Jill clearly identified her mental picture of God. We began by closing our eyes and setting a prayerful intention.

"Jill, what do you see in your mind's eye?" I asked. "Is there an image or picture of God?"

Comfortable with the silence, we gave God time and space to move.

"Yes," she said, quietly. "He is sitting on a throne in an embroidered robe. The throne is high with a big staircase in front of it."

"Do you sense any emotions? What might the atmosphere in that space feel like to you?" I asked.

"Oh, cold. It feels very cold," she said. "And there is a big Plexiglas divider between us. I can see through it, but I can't get through it to God. It's a big barrier, a divider. It's keeping me out. It feels scary and uncomfortable."

"Can you describe the countenance of God?" I asked, curious as to why she felt scared and uncomfortable.

Tears began falling down her face. "He is frowning. Harsh and almost . . . mean. I know I shouldn't say that—He's God, and I should respect Him, no matter what. I should be okay with that."

"That's a lot of shoulds," I said.

In our remaining time together, I discovered that Jill had been through a very tough church split with her family. She'd been in her late teens, and this church was her second home. At the core of the division, dissension, and tremendous disheartening negativity was the priest, dearly beloved by Jill. He was a father image, and someone she deeply trusted. And, yes, on Sundays and for special church celebrations, he dressed in embroidered robes.

More often than not, our mental image of God is dressed as either someone we deeply love, someone who perhaps has deeply wounded us, or even some *place*—a setting or geographic location, as in my journey with the nuns and the lonely white line. My perception of God had been shaped by a rigid, austere nun who'd punished a sweet-natured, vivacious, relational little girl by publicly disciplining her for talking too much.

As we probe to answer Tozer's revelatory question, "What comes to mind when we think about God?" we clarify our question, "Do I think God is trustworthy?" One answer informs the other and helps us set aside unhealthy, false beliefs in order to live out healthy, true beliefs.

Kiss the Clouds

A funny thing happened in the middle—or was it at the end?—of my frightening free fall. Suddenly, everything changed. Remember that parachute I totally forgot about? Unbeknownst to me, Tandem Jim released the pilot chute and deceleration happened. In a millisecond, we went from spiraling to our deaths to floating in the clouds. It seems the little white pilot chute acts as an anchor in the air. It usually takes three to five seconds from deployment of the pilot chute to full inflation of the canopy. Shortly after, the closing pin of the pilot chute releases the main chute, and all is well with the world.

Tandem Jim tapped my arm and motioned for me to take the reins of the parachute.

Oh no. I shook my head. *I am fine right here.* Before the jump, I was bent on taking control, thinking how great that would be. I learned real fast that I was perfectly fine letting the master run the show.

With gentleness and kindness, he said, "Then lean back on me. Take it all in. We're going to go left"—he guided us left—"now we're going to go right"—and he guided us right.

The peace was truly one that passed understanding. There we were. Floating on a cushion of thin air.

He then said the most beautiful thing. "Kiss the clouds."

As we moved through the white cumulus clouds, he said it again, "Kiss the clouds."

Soaring through those clouds revived me. In preparing for the jump, I had thought the skydive was to prove my research, but in that moment, I saw that it was to awaken my spirit. The crushing season had left me numb and listless. Maybe you know exactly what I am talking about. Unnerving feelings I never want to feel again. After a long, hard season of pain, I think I just needed to feel something . . . anything . . . again. I wanted to feel alive. Kissing the clouds at ten thousand feet in the air offered an entirely different perspective for the rest of my life. From this elevated vantage point, everything below looked small and incidental. That, and that alone, stirs my soul from any thought of numbness today. It reminds me that God is bigger than any hurtful words that come my way.

Tandem Jim became the perfect living model of the threefold cord of trusting in God: trustworthy, dependable, and safe.

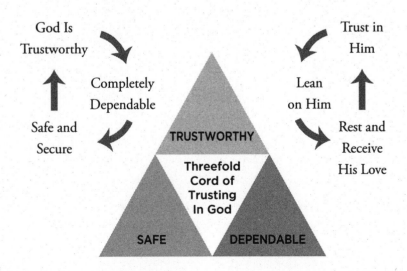

I Will Be Sure Always

Right before Tandem Jim and I approached our safe and soft landing, I remembered the conversation I'd had earlier in the week with a retired army jumpmaster, Frank, who shared with me the motto of an army parachute rigger: "I will be sure always."[82]

I will be sure always. As I meditated on these five words, I found a renewed impetus to put my trust in God. *I will be sure always* is such an empowering statement, so confident and so undeniably forthright. Just saying the words aloud gives energy. Try it.

I will be sure always.

As Frank and I had continued our conversation, he shared these thoughts, memorized from years of training. The words were so powerful that I went straight to the manual myself and copied them, word for word. "At jump school, you'll be introduced to your best friend—your parachute. You'll get to know everything about it. How to wear it, adjust it, use it, the works. You'll always learn all the techniques needed to accomplish your mission with absolute confidence. How to stay loose; get ready for impact; let your legs absorb the shock; roll and collapse your chute quickly; release your harness; unsling your weapon; and deploy your position."[83]

Finally, after arduous training protocol, every parachute rigger raises their right hand and takes the Rigger's Pledge upon completion of their training:

- I will keep constantly in mind that until men grow wings, their parachutes must be dependable.
- I will pack every parachute as though I am to jump with it myself and will stand ready to jump with any parachute that I have certified as properly packed.

- I will remember always that the other man's life is as dear to him as mine is to me.
- I will never resort to guesswork, as I know that chance is a fool's gold and that I, a rigger, cannot depend on it.
- I will never pass over any defect nor neglect any repair, no matter how small, as I know that omissions and mistakes in the rigging of a parachute may cost a life.
- I will keep all parachute equipment entrusted to my care in the best possible condition, remembering always that the little things left undone cause major troubles.
- I will never sign my name to a parachute inspection or packing certificate unless I have personally performed or directly supervised every step and am entirely satisfied with all the work.
- I will never let the idea that a piece of work is "good enough" make me a potential murderer through a careless mistake or oversight, for I know there can be no compromise with perfection.
- I will keep always a wholehearted respect for my vocation, regarding it as a high profession rather than a day-to-day task, and will keep in mind constantly my grave responsibility.
- I will be sure always.[84]

The Heartlifter's Pledge

The words of that pledge quickened my spirit, and suddenly the spiritual principles and parallels crystallized. Everything Frank had shared with me boiled down to rigorous, repetitive skill building and high levels of trust—both physically and mentally.

This sounds so familiar to the practices of our heartlift journey.

You have new tools: nine healthy practices, WHOLE, a new language of love that involves both tough and tender behaviors (emotional regulation, establishing boundaries, healthy cognition, sound belief systems, and holistic self-care and self-compassion) and spiritual truths that will enliven and empower you.

What if we took a similar pledge? Let's boldly proclaim our Heartlifter's Pledge and say with newfound boldness:

- God is trustworthy; I will be sure always (Hebrews 13:8).
- I will believe that in every situation, God is dependable and trustworthy (Romans 8:28).
- I will stand ready to serve God at any time and in any place (Matthew 24:44).
- I will count other's lives as more important than my own (Philippians 2:3).
- I will never resort to guesswork, but believe wholeheartedly in the Word of God (Psalm 18:30).
- I will daily attend to the spiritual disciplines of study, meditation, and prayer; for I know that the little things left undone cause major troubles (Psalm 119:10).
- I will honor God with my work, giving 100 percent to all He has called me to do (Ecclesiastes 9:10).
- I will strive for perfection (spiritual maturity and emotional health) in all I do (Matthew 5:48).
- I will press toward the high calling of Christ Jesus, keeping in mind my grave responsibility to finish the race God has set before me (Philippians 3:14).
- I will be sure always: God is trustworthy (Psalm 9:9–10). Amen.

At the end of the day, believing that God is trustworthy and placing our trust in Him is a huge leap of faith, but each of us will have to take that daunting leap alone. I cannot crawl into your heart and own your pain. It is yours. I can have compassion, empathy, and a certain degree of understanding, but your walk is yours and my walk is mine. You must walk through it—you and your God. I can walk beside you, pray for you, call back with encouraging words, and ultimately assure you of God's love, but you must place your trust in God yourself. I can't trust in God for you.

If I can offer you anything from my own heartlift journey, it is this one truth: No one else can ever understand your journey. It is highly personal, deeply unique, and intentionally designed by God. Just look at our word, *trust*. What sits in the middle? *Us*. He holds your heart in His loving hands, and He is exacting in His execution of its journey. It is about "us."

Oswald Chambers, author of famed devotional *My Utmost for His Highest*, boldly wrote:

> The Holy Spirit may call us to a definite purpose for our life and we know that it means a decision, a reckless fling over onto God, a burning of our bridges behind us, and there is not a soul to advise us when we take that step except the Holy Spirit. Our clinging comes in this way: We put one foot on God's side and one on the side of human reasoning. Then God widens the space until we either drop between or jump to the other side. We have to take a leap—a reckless leap—and if we have learned to rely on the Holy Spirit, it will be a reckless leap to God's side.[85]

Maybe you find yourself standing on the edge of that reckless leap, toes gripping the sharp edge, heart pounding at a frightening pace, palms sweating with heightened anxiety, mind racing with competing thoughts. Take the leap . . . don't take the leap. Trust again . . . don't trust again. If so, I'm here with you. Take my hand. Together, we'll take that God-sized breath, be filled up with our Genesis 2:7 value, worth, and dignity, and take that reckless leap to God's side. He is waiting for us on the other side. Arms open, God assures His presence, "You've got this, child, you can trust again."

HEART CARE

Reflect:
Prayer, the Great Decelerator

Let's talk about those times in our lives when we feel as though we've been pushed out of an airplane. Times when the gravity of hurtful words has taken our breath away, and we feel like we are in a free fall. I find it interesting that free fall is defined as "falling under the sole influence of gravity" and that "all freefalling objects accelerate downward at a very fast rate—9.8 m/s/s to be exact."[86] In your time of reflection, consider this question: "Do we not fall under the sole force of gravity when hurtful words are spoken?" We'll define gravity, here, as "seriousness, magnitude, significance, or importance."[87]

Psychologists call this emotional response as "fear, panic" or oftentimes, "a panic attack."[88] Two words describe panic: sudden and extreme. Rooted in fear, panic wreaks havoc on the nervous system. What can you do to slow down the acceleration of panic in those grave moments? You can deploy the parachute of prayer.

In our lectio divina way, place yourself right in the middle of Deuteronomy 20:1–4 (MSG), personalizing this spiritual directive:

When you go to war against your enemy and see horses and chariots and soldiers far outnumbering you, do not recoil in fear of them; GOD, your God, who brought you up out of Egypt is with you. When the battle is about to begin, let the priest come forward and speak to the troops. He'll say, "Attention, Israel. In a few minutes, you're going to do battle with your enemies. Don't waver in resolve. Don't fear.

Don't hesitate. Don't panic. GOD, your God, is right there with you, fighting with you against your enemies, fighting to win."

Further, the apostle Paul reminds us in Ephesians 6:12 (NKJV) that

We do not wrestle against flesh and blood, but against principalities, against powers, against the rulers of the darkness of this age, against spiritual hosts of wickedness in the heavenly places.

People are not our enemies—the principalities and powers of darkness behind them are. Keeping this in the forefront of our minds reduces our need to hate, retaliate, or even wish vengeance upon others. To help me understand this, I've turned to Paul's words in Romans 12:9: "Love must be sincere. Hate what is evil; cling to what is good." *Good* here means "useful and beneficial,"[89] and *cling* means "to glue together; cement."[90] The visual is so clear. We don't condone the evil. Rather, we glue ourselves to people, places, and resources that are useful and beneficial. This will keep us in the light, where love and truth grow.

Reframe

As the parachute deployed and panic gave way to peace, I remembered that I was holding little pieces of paper in my hand. Before the jump, I'd set an intention to put into practice the words of Hebrews 12:1–2, "Therefore, since we are surrounded by such a great cloud of witnesses, let us throw off everything that hinders and the sin that so easily entangles. And let us run [or can I say free fall?] with persever-ance the race marked out for us, fixing our eyes on Jesus, the pioneer and perfecter of our faith." The King James Version actually says we are "looking unto Jesus, the author and finisher of our faith."

I wanted to "throw off everything that hinders," and so I wrote down the hurtful words that had been spoken over me. Every single significant word. They had entangled me long enough. It was time for them to go. My sister had added hers. Once I remembered, I said a quick good-bye prayer and let them go. It was a symbolic gesture, but it held eternal power for me.

What do you need to write down on a little piece of paper and let go? Maybe you'll experience an actual free fall, too, but it certainly isn't necessary. Am I sensing a sigh of relief? Don't worry. Instead, be creative. I've had clients write on bricks and throw them into the river. A friend uses rice paper—then dips it into water and watches it dissolve.

Reauthor

Tozer's question, "What comes to mind when you think about God?" is quite important. Take your time as you move through these guid-ing questions:

- What are your earliest recollections of God? Church? Faith? Spirituality?
- Is your idea of God hindered by notions of religious rituals instead of authentic relationship with God?
- How have those recollections and notions authored your per-ceptions and belief systems?
- Does your belief system need to be reauthored?

Smile at Your Future

The Intention of Practice 9:
I will overcome hurtful words by smiling
at the remarkable future in front of me.

If you don't take responsibility for living your God-given life,
it will not get lived. There is no one else in the world like you.
No one! One of the greatest ways you can honor and glorify God
is through embracing your unrepeatable life.
—GERI SCAZZERO[91]

On the last evening of a weekend getaway, my daughter, Candace, and I decided to go for a final walk on the beach. With threatening storm clouds moving our way, we knew time was of the essence. Ten minutes into the walk, a light rain began to fall.

"Mom, let's turn around," she said. "It's raining. You have an iPhone in your hand. It shouldn't get wet, right?"

Stubborn at first, I prodded her to keep going. For some reason, she persisted.

"No, we need to turn back," she said again. This resistance

seemed so odd coming from a fearless, female travel writer whose job has caused her to endure far more than a few raindrops.

We turned around, but by the time we reached our starting point, the rain had stopped. It was as if God held the clouds still. My daughter changed her mind.

"Mom, let's keep going this way," she urged. "I know how much you want to take one last walk on your favorite beach."

We were as indecisive as the sand crabs crisscrossing our path as they raced from their holes to the water and back again. A few feet into our revived walk, I saw in the distance a group of women, their beach chairs arranged in a half moon on the sand.

"I wonder what they're doing?" I said curiously.

"I bet they are having a book club," Candace said, noting the books on their laps. As writers, nothing could make our hearts happier. I walked over to them to snap a photo. I'm not really sure why, but my heart leapt when I saw them.

Sauntering up with the greatest respect, I caught their attention. "Excuse me," I said. "Would you mind if I took your picture?"

"Oh, sure!" they exclaimed, and adjusted their chairs, drawing in a little closer.

"Is this a book club?" I asked.

"No, this is a Bible study," they chimed as each raised her book simultaneously. "We actually call ourselves a community group."

"Truth be told, I am a writer, and I'm here working on a book about the hurtful words women speak to one another."

Their faces lit up like Times Square.

"No way," they exclaimed, looking at one another in disbelief. "You've got to be kidding. We were just talking about that. We want that book. Come back when it is all done, please!"

Within seconds, we were fast friends. I ran around the circle, high-fiving as if the clock had just struck midnight on New Year's Eve. Some might call this a God-thing, or a God-wink. I called it a smile from God. Yes, ma'am—there on an ordinary beach, God smiled, right at me.

I felt as if I were ten feet off the ground.

After a few more moments of exchanging emails and phone numbers with the leader of the group, Candace and I walked on.

Suddenly, I realized something. This was the exact beach town where my Angela encounter had happened. As we've learned on this journey, God cares about location—settings and geography. He goes to great lengths to heal the pain locked inside our hearts. Like with Mack in *The Shack*, sometimes God takes us back to the place where we got stuck in our pain. It might seem cruel and uncaring at first, but ultimately, it is deep and freeing. This is how God takes care of His children. He loves us deeply and will go to any length to show us how much (Luke 15:4–7).

Filled with gratitude, my daughter and I kept walking. "Well, that was mighty special," she said, knowing all too well her mother's history of hurts.

I smiled. "It sure was."

When we left our little getaway and drove home, we came to the same bridge I had crossed over four years earlier. I pulled the car over for a moment, just to take pause. To give God thanks. I found myself praying.

God, four years ago, right here on this bridge, I asked You to help me. I had two choices before me. I could listen to the lies and drive off the bridge of life, or I could listen to the truth and build a bridge of hope and healing for hurting women like myself. Thank You for helping me, Father. Today, we begin writing the new narrative. Amen.

As we crossed the bridge to go home, I felt my smile making its way to my heart. I felt free and loved and ready to move on.

It's Time to Cross Your Bridge

Tucked at the end of the book of Proverbs is the profile of a remarkable, heartlifting woman. Known through the centuries as the Proverbs 31 woman, she has often gotten a bad rap. *She is perfect. I could never be like her. Model Christian. Gourmet chef. Real estate tycoon. Emotional rock. Social activist. Seamstress extraordinaire. Married well. Pillar in her community. Parented honor students. Yep, perfection. Not for me.*

I'll admit, she is a little intimidating if—and this is a big if—you forget this woman is not real! The mother of a king jotted this "inspired utterance" as a standard of excellence by which her son should look for a queen (Proverbs 31:10–31). We might call this proverbial woman a standard-bearer or a role model in today's vernacular. Someone to look up to and aspire to be like.

I call her a bridge.

Several years ago, I read these beautiful words from Oprah Winfrey. "I am where I am today," she writes, "because of the bridges that I crossed. Harriet Tubman was a bridge. Sojourner Truth was a bridge."[92] She proceeds to note all of the women who had served as bridges in her life. I love her choice of metaphor because bridges serve as a means "of allowing passage across some obstacle."[93]

The proverbial woman, fiction or not, showed up in my life at just the right time. Isn't it funny how that happens? While mosey-ing around one of my favorite retail therapy stores, I turned down one long aisle, and there it was, shining like a masterpiece in an art gallery—an eighteen-by-twenty-four-inch chocolate-brown can-vas with this proverbial wisdom beautifully scripted in ivory font: "Clothed in strength and dignity, with nothing to fear, she smiles when she thinks about the future" (Proverbs 31:25).

I had a moment. Maybe two. I stood there as if I were in Paris, looking at the *Mona Lisa* in the Louvre. These mesmerizing words seemed like the perfect beginning for my new narrative. Words hurt and words heal. There really is no in-between. They hold life and death in their hands (Proverbs 18:21). Sometimes they taste as sweet as a honeycomb (Proverbs 16:24), and sometimes they wield as much power as a sword (Proverbs 12:18). The words of Proverbs 31:25 seized my heart and became a deep, life-giving, even prophetic foot-ing for the rest of my life, reauthoring the negative narrative. *Today, I am clothed in strength and dignity. Today, I have nothing to fear. Today, I smile when I think of the future.*

I claimed that art as my own, paid far less than I would a da Vinci original, brought it home, and positioned it on my dining room wall where every person who walks into my home can see it. The message is that important to me.

Clothed in Strength and Dignity

During my heartrifting journey, I'd suffered with mystifying bouts of acute chest pain (radiating upward into the jaw), shortness of breath, mental fatigue, and gastrointestinal issues. Tests were run, medica-tions prescribed, and simple "watch-and-sees" given. At the time, I thought it was stress induced. A great deal was going on in my life (which isn't unusual), so I chalked it up to my normal grab-life-with-gusto and kept going.

The conditions didn't go away, but I seemed to be managing them with regular exercise and the stress-relieving tactics I know to do. But then, something entirely new happened.

I began having swallowing issues. First a serious choking incident and then progressive difficulty in swallowing—to the point that even drinking water became problematic. Shortness of breath came with bouts of intense upper-back pain and deep spasms, which presented much like a heart attack. After teaching or talking for any length of time, my voice would be hoarse and I was utterly exhausted. When simple changes didn't work, my doctor suggested a specialist. Because my mother and daughter had both recently undergone brain surgeries, he wanted to make sure my little brain was okay. Over the next several months, I endured a series of tests for various maladies. Finally, a new and improved test, an esophageal manometry, was scheduled.

A few days after the test, my doctor's nurse called. "Janell, Dr. Lawson would like to schedule an appointment for you to come in and discuss your options."

"Options?" I asked. "That doesn't sound good."

"Well, the manometry concluded you have a rare esophageal disease called *achalasia*," she said.

"Excuse me, ache-a-what?" I repeated. "I'm sorry, what did you say? Could you please spell that for me?" I grabbed pen and paper and started writing.

She proceeded to spell it out, a-c-h-a-l-a-s-i-a, but all I heard was f-e-a-r. Fear snuck right in and sat on one shoulder. Faith walked in and sat on the other. Thankfully, Faith's voice was much louder, as she reminded me of my new narrative: "You are clothed in strength and dignity, with nothing to fear. Remember that."

With Nothing to Fear

The scary in-between began with all its Google searching, fear-laden onslaught of questions, and unanswered concerns. I wanted answers and quick fixes and simple solutions. I wanted to stand in a prayer line and get healed. Instead—you guessed it—I found myself sitting in yet another waiting room, literally. As usual, I had to wait quite a while for the doctor. But as we've discovered, something quite magical happens in that quiet, often isolated space.

Things slow down. We get quiet. The tyranny of the urgent becomes the vitality of the here and now. Sitting in that room, I practiced what I preach and welcomed God into the whys.

You are welcome here, God. You are welcome.

I wrote one word in my heart journal: *Achalasia*. And then I prayed, "God, speak through my doctor and help me to both listen and hear Your voice within his voice. Amen."

When the doctor came in, he apologized for the wait.

"No worries," I said. "You gave me time to think. To get some work done. It's so quiet in here."

He smiled. "Well, that's good. What are you working on?"

I smiled back. "It's kind of ironic. I was reworking a piece on being blindsided by something and the temptation to ask, 'Why did that just happen?'" I remarked that he might end up in that piece.

The conversation that followed was a sincere future-changer. His words remain a marker on my life map.

"You will need surgery. I'd like to send you to Johns Hopkins for a medical consult on the brand-new peroral endoscopic myotomy surgical procedure. It's also called the POEM procedure. Probably less than one hundred people have had it, worldwide. We will set up an appointment with the best surgeon in the area to discuss all your options." He continued talking about medical dispensations and high risks and nerves and valves and . . .

My head was spinning like a top. My heart was sinking, but I kept welcoming God into my whirlwind of whys, hows, whats, and whos.

You are welcome here, God. Very welcome.

"Dr. Lawson, what did I do to cause this? I know I've been under a great deal of stress. There must be something I can do to fix it. Some natural things, right? Change my diet? Change my personality? Change my vocation? Do something calmer? Quieter? Move to a small town? Anything?"

"Listen, write this down in that little notebook of yours," he said firmly, like a good father. "This is not your fault. There are things in life that you don't control, and this is one of them. There is no evidence or research that gives the reason for this disease. Only supposition. Perhaps with the continued advancement of the manometry test, more can be discovered. Some researchers indicate it may come from the measles virus. That's all we have."

"Well, that is really hard to accept," I said, fighting back a big, ugly cry. "There has to be something I can do."

"Let me repeat myself," he said, this time moving his chair directly in front of me. "I'm afraid not. Nothing you did caused this."

"So, you just wake up one morning and there it is . . . *boom!* Achalasia?" I said.

"Yes, achalasia chose you. And I know for a fact that, at the end of this journey, you will be an expert on the subject."

It's Time to Burn a Bridge

He was right. Achalasia was a future-changer. I did become an expert, especially about swallowing, both physically and emotionally. I became hypervigilant about this highly underestimated human function. I leaned in hard to hear the whispers of God. The more I read and the more I prayed, the more I saw a direct link between my inability to swallow and my unhealthy capacity to suppress negative emotions. One aspect of the word *swallow* is "to suppress feelings."[94] If we take it one step further, as we've learned to do on our journey, we will see that *suppress* means "to resist something consciously."[95] Behavioral scientists report that "repressers," or people who "maintain a stiff upper lip under all circumstances, are one of the most mystifying personality types. The represser's calm is bought at a great price."[96] Dr. Daniel Weinberger, psychologist at Stanford University, adds, "Over time, the represser's style of stifling reactions tends to take a toll on health."[97]

Very strong words, those—*stifle, repress, suppress*. Learned, unhealthy behaviors that this girl knew didn't belong in her new narrative.

I am clothed in strength and dignity, with nothing to stifle. With nothing to suppress. With nothing to repress.

"Sometimes the best light," writes American singer-songwriter Don Henley, "comes from a burning bridge."[98] Without even knowing it, Dr. Lawson helped me burn a bridge. The light of his expertise and empathy ushered in my new narrative, which involved not swallowing unhealthy, negative emotions—my own or anybody else's.

Months later, I had the POEM experimental surgery. I was the third person in Virginia to do so, and I am happy to say it was successful. It's a palliative treatment, not curative, but it helped, nonetheless. This future-changer created a new normal, for sure, and daily reminds me to clothe myself in strength and dignity—to remember whose I am and who I am.

It's Time to Build an Emotional Bridge

Sheryl is a proverbial woman who smiles and often laughs at the future. At a time when I needed her most, she became an emotional bridge in my life.

One Sunday morning, as I moved through the crowded corridor at church, my arm brushed hers. I looked up to see Sheryl's smiling face. We'd spoken here and there, but never at any great length. In a big church, Sunday mornings are often just pass-by hellos and simple exchanges of "How are you?" and "I hope you have a great week." Everyone is busy getting to class or picking up their children. Time spent in deep conversations is rare.

"Janell! Hi! I am so glad I bumped into you. I've been wanting to ask you something," Sheryl said. Without taking a breath, she continued. "Would you be interested in going to Kenya to do a women's retreat for the mamas of our Joy Village? We've never done anything like this before, but we're thinking it's the right time. I can't think of anyone better to lead our first Mamas' Retreat than you. What do you think?"

A bit stunned yet over-the-moon happy, I immediately exclaimed, "Yes! Yes! Yes!" And then I collected myself and said I'd definitely have to run it by my husband. Tears started flowing. "You know, Sheryl, today is exactly six months from my POEM surgery. I don't think this is a coincidence."

"Well, you've got a few more months to heal up," she said. "Kenya is calling."

And Kenya *was* calling—calling me to build the bridge of hope and healing I'd said yes to at the beginning of my heartlift journey.

At some point on your journey through this book, have you whispered a yes to something inside your heart? Something you thought might never happen? Today is your day to smile at your future. To write the first word of your new narrative. Maybe you could start it with this: "God is calling. I have a few more months to heal up, but God is calling."

Crossing the Great Rift Valley

Hurtful words are future-changers, but within their heartrifting fury, God hides a divine invitation to true freedom in Christ. Wrapped in their intentional pain, they have one goal: to keep a good woman down. There is nothing that gives the enemy of our soul greater satisfaction. But we have joined forces and decided that we will not let this happen. Together—because we are so much better together—we have rallied and risen and received an enlarged capacity to overcome any sly, oppressive, and sometimes overt attempts at keeping us down. My best friend, Sandy, gave me a plaque that I keep at eye level in my office. It reads, "Be the kind of woman that when your feet hit the floor each morning, the devil says, 'Oh no, she's up!'"

I met nine women in Kenya, each one called "mama" by six to twelve children, who can make the devil say, "Oh no, she's up!" Every morning, these ladies wake up at 5:00 a.m. Within minutes, they are cooking, serving, and getting all those children prepared for school. Morning devotionals and earnest prayer are a big part of that routine. Each woman sacrifices her time and energy to live on the grounds of the Joy Village in order to make a home for these children. Varying circumstances have brought each child to this haven, but here they find love, safety, and immense joy. In just the one night I spent with Mama Elizabeth, I saw personally the rigors of their daily routine. After only eight hours, I was exhausted. As a mama myself, I understood on some level, yet I have far more conveniences (and far fewer children) at hand to help. I couldn't wait to be part of blessing her and the other mamas with three days of "pampering with a purpose"—creating space for each of them to experience the power of a heartlift.

En route from our home base, Nazareth Hospital in Limuru, to the retreat center in Lake Naivasha, we crossed through the Great Rift Valley. Yes, the Great *Rift* Valley. You read that right! Once again, the God who sees was guiding our journey, down to the smallest of details. As I looked out the window and across the great expanse of valley—Mount Longonot standing tall like a Masai warrior in the distance—I was completely overwhelmed by the goodness of God. What-ifs filled the Kenyan air swirling about the van. Each bump in the road resounded with what-ifs. *What if I had quit on all this? What if I had let the negative power of those hurtful words stall my destiny? What if the grudges and grief had waylaid me on the way here?*

I looked into the faces of the women in the van. Each woman had made her own separate journey to be part of this inaugural retreat. Crossing the Great Rift Valley felt like a rite of passage—transitioning from a season of crushing heartrifts to a new season of offering heartlifts. They would no longer be entangled in hurtful words but embraced by healthy hearts, committed to creating a healthy community.

Bridges Help Us Become Our Best

Bridges in our lives help us overcome the obstacles placed in our path so that we can become our very best self. They connect us to every necessary resource, and with them, we can cross the Great Rift Valleys of our lives and move forward into our God-breathed capacity, potential, and powerful destiny. Our enemy's oppressive attempts to keep good women down backfires in his face because, in his futile attempt, our united front is impossible to penetrate. When women gather in the indomitable spirit of unity, the gates of hell cannot prevail. The more the enemy tries to push us down, the more we rise above and commit to becoming our best.

Author Tim Duncan writes, "Good, better, best. Never let it rest. Until your good is better and your better is best."[99] The apostle Paul says it this way: "Earnestly desire the best gifts. And yet I show you a more excellent way" (1 Corinthians 12:31 NKJV). As the meaning of the little superlative "best" unfolded before me, all I could do was smile. It summarizes absolutely everything I hope for you—that this heartlifting journey has brought you to a better place and invited you to become your very best self. I think you'll be as surprised as I was when you see the potency of what Paul was really praying.

| Best[100] | Translated from Greek, *kreitton*, means "more useful, more serviceable, more advantageous, and more excellent." |
| | Root of kreitton, *kratos*, means "force, strength, and mighty in power." |

Excellent[101]	Translated from Greek, root, *hyperbole*, means "a throwing beyond others; beyond measure, exceedingly, superiority."
Way[102]	Translated from Greek, *hodos*, means "a traveller's way; a way of thinking, feeling, deciding."

When Paul urges us to "desire the best gifts," he is asking that we pray for gifts that are "more useful, more serviceable, more advantageous, and more excellent." And in doing so, we will be exceedingly blessed with the strength to do mighty deeds with power.

When Paul states, "I will show you a more excellent way," he is promising resources that exceed and go beyond the measure of the norm, so that our way of thinking, feeling, and deciding will be filled with the knowledge and truth of God's ways and words (Matthew 22:16).

No longer do I tritely use the phrase "I wish you the best." Instead, it has become a powerful proclamation I use wisely. I've also grown in my understanding that it isn't important to be *the best*, but to become *my best*. Living in this profound truth alleviates the need to compete with other women, to strive for perfection, or to climb any type of ladder of success or notoriety. Perhaps that is why I now consider Angela one of my bridges. She helped me cross over so many obstacles and, in doing so, helped me move into "a more excellent way."

Letting the More Excellent Way Unfold

While sitting in a circle, listening to thundering rain fall on the tin roof above us, the more excellent way unfolded. On the first day of the Kenyan Mamas' Retreat, we set up the conference room much like we would here in the States. Long, rectangular tables arranged in a U shape and covered with white tablecloths, retreat packets neatly placed, ready for each woman to sit and learn. Podium for the teacher.

After the first session, Sheryl came to me. "It just doesn't feel right," she said. "It's too formal. I think we should come up with another plan. I'm sensing water. Something with water."

"Water?" I asked, knowing that I had all the sessions planned and ready. Water wasn't anywhere on the agenda. "Okay, water. Let's see what we can do."

I scanned the room. There was a pitcher of ice water with glasses. *That could work.*

I looked outside. There was a pool with tables and sun umbrellas. *That could work.*

We walked the grounds, on the hunt for the best place to gather. Within minutes, it started to pour. Water in the form of raindrops. Big, juicy raindrops. *Hmmm . . . we definitely have water now.*

"Outside is not the best option," I said. But then, I saw it. A building beside the pool that had an outside area under a tin roof. Just a slab of concrete, but it had potential. And it was covered. We would be dry.

"That's it," we agreed. We gathered multicolored plastic chairs, put them in a circle, placed a vase of stunning Kenyan roses in the center, and found our new home. The simplicity of the area invited intimacy, authenticity, and stillness. With all reverence and honor to the word *holy*, a slab of concrete became a sacred place and holy ground. I didn't want to be anywhere else.

The team huddled to seek what God might have in store. Trusting Sheryl's innate sense to hear from the Spirit, we talked about what might be done with a pitcher of ice water.

"I've got it," chimed Judy, our resident licensed professional counselor. "There is a really beautiful spoken blessing exercise I've used in the past. Every woman's name is written on a piece of paper and placed in a basket. Then, each is given an empty glass, holding it before her. The first woman draws a name from the basket, takes the pitcher of water, stands in front of the woman whose name she has drawn, and then pours water into the glass while pronouncing a spoken blessing over her. It's as simple as, 'Your radiant smile lights up the room. It is evident God has given you the gift of joy. Share this with everyone in your life. Light up their darkness.' This continues until every woman has experienced a blessing."

One by one, the blessings unfolded as the glasses and hearts were filled. Hearing words of life spoken over each woman increased my passion for the power of unity. Here were fifteen women with one beautiful beating heart, sitting in a circle of unity. It didn't matter that we were from two completely different continents, two very different cultures, and two distinct races—we had one united purpose: to bless one another.

The evening closed with a deeply moving foot-washing service, where once again, we sat in a circle of unity. With the lights dim and hearts quiet, we brought the words of Jesus in John 13:12–17 to this simple room:

> When he had finished washing their feet, he put on his clothes and returned to his place. "Do you understand what I have done for you?" he asked them. "You call me 'Teacher' and 'Lord,' and rightly so, for that is what I am. Now that I, your Lord and Teacher, have washed your feet, you also should wash one another's feet. I have set you an example

that you should do as I have done for you. Very truly I tell you, no servant is greater than his master, nor is a messenger greater than the one who sent him. Now that you know these things, you will be blessed if you do them."

Heartlifters Unite

Unity simply means "oneness." Paul, while sitting in prison, offered these thoughts in his letter to the Ephesian church:

As a prisoner for the Lord, then, I urge you to live a life worthy of the calling you have received. Be completely humble and gentle; be patient, bearing with one another in love. Make every effort to keep the unity of the Spirit through the bond of peace. There is one body and one Spirit, just as you were called to one hope when you were called; one Lord, one faith, one baptism; one God and Father of all, who is over all and through all and in all.

—Ephesians 4:1–6

The poetic language of this prayer takes my breath away. Note the repetitive use of the word *one*: one body, one Spirit, one hope, one Lord, one faith, one baptism, and one God, and how strongly it signals the way Paul felt about the issue of unity among the community of Christ followers. He knew the great difficulty, yet he still put forth the challenge. He knew unity wouldn't come naturally; we must work at both obtaining and maintaining it.

Paul's beautiful reflection of the Father in the Son and the Son in us works almost like a child's butterfly mirror painting, in which paint from one side of a piece of paper is transferred to the other by folding the sheet in half. Paul's desire for unity leaves me longing to see this happen in our lives as well, that the unity of the Father and Son will be transferred into our daily relationships just like a mirror painting. Why does he want believers, both present and future, to express complete unity? So they can be a witness to the world of the overwhelming, unconditional love that God has for every being on earth.

Jesus, in His final prayer here on earth, voiced His passion for unity:

> I pray also for those who will believe in me through their message, that all of them may be one, Father, just as you are in me and I am in you. May they also be in us so that the world may believe that you have sent me. I have given them the glory that you gave me, that they may be one as we are one—I in them and you in me—so that they may be brought to complete unity. Then the world will know that you sent me and have loved them even as you have loved me.
> —John 17:20–23

Smile at Your Future

If I could, I'd gather as many multicolored plastic chairs as I could find, place them in one very large circle, and have us all sit down together. Maybe one day that can happen. Until then, I am going to bless you, right here and now. Wherever you are, please have a seat with me. I'm placing a beautiful vase of Kenyan roses on a table right in the middle of our circle. Can you smell them? See their radiant blooms? Now I am placing a crystal glass in your hand. I've drawn your name and so am ready to proclaim a blessing over you. Read this aloud with me:

Today is no ordinary day. Today, you cross through the Great Rift Valley, leaving every hurtful word behind. Today, a community of remarkable heartlifters, committed to a more excellent way, welcomes you with open hands and united hearts. Together— because we are so much better together—this community commits to helping others experience the power of a heartlift. You've overcome the hurtful words spoken over you—or are well on your way to doing so—and are living in the beautiful promise of Proverbs 31:25 (VOICE), "Clothed in strength and dignity, with nothing to fear, she smiles when she thinks about the future."

HEART CARE

Reflect

In lectio divina fashion, read through Proverbs 31:10–31, preferably using the Amplified translation of the Bible, which offers insights and meaning to the literal usage of the words. Remember the proverbial woman is but a standard-bearer. A role model. A healthy, emotional bridge. Who are your healthy emotional bridges? Following Oprah's model, which we will lovingly call "Crossings," create a record of your crossings—the healthy, emotional bridges women have helped you navigate on your healing journey. Noting these "crossings" is a beautiful gratitude exercise that helps us see just how far we've come.

Here's an example to help you get started:
I am where I am today because of the emotional bridges that I crossed. Kristine was an emotional bridge. She helped me see the unhealthy behavior patterns in my relationships and definitely helped me recognize my faulty thinking patterns.

_____ was an emotional bridge. She helped me _____.

_____ was an emotional bridge. She helped me _____.

_____ was an emotional bridge. She helped me _____.

_____ was an emotional bridge. She helped me _____.

_____ was an emotional bridge. She helped me _____.

Reframe

Read the following excerpt from *The Healing Power of Dialogue*, by Masao Yokota:

> Clearly, dialogue is more than ordinary conversation. The purpose of dialogue is to understand others—not just to share our independent views. That would limit our exchange to information and dialogue is not just about information. In a dialogue, we have a responsibility to be present and enrich each other. We should always remember that the words *respond* and *responsibility* come from the Latin word *respondere*, which means "promise." This kind of communication is not natural for human beings because humans are basically selfish and self-centered. This reality makes it especially difficult to conduct dialogue in a talking and teaching culture; communication is easier in a listening and learning culture. So, sometimes we must develop our skills in order to be capable of dialogue. Patience is needed but that is not the most difficult thing; what can be more difficult is developing an appropriate attitude, a deep awareness of others. This is what allows us to create harmony.[103]

In light of these words, practice the healing dialogue in your community. When women gather, words flow. Embrace your new-found sense of security and strength by guiding women in healthy, heartlifting conversations. Celebrate the gifts and talents of others. Begin the Ephesians 4:29 way of life: "Do not let any unwholesome talk come out of your mouths, but only what is helpful for building others up according to their needs, that it may benefit those who listen."

Reauthor

The words of the Proverbs 31 woman offered me a deep, life-giving, prophetic footing for my new narrative, "clothed in strength and dignity, with nothing to fear, she smiles when she thinks about the future" (Proverb 31:25 VOICE). Prophetic footing means you have "a base for your progress."[104] A strong, stable foundation on which you can build the rest of your life.

You have read many words on this heartlifting journey. Are there any that have given you prophetic footing—a base for *your* new narrative? Perhaps as you take time to sit in your beautiful waiting room, those words will come. I can't wait to hear all about it.

Endnotes

Practice 1: *Guard Your Heart*

1. Stein, Joel. "Nip. Tuck. Or Else." *Time* Magazine, June 15, 2015, 40–48.
2. Ibid.
3. "Guide to Reading Microexpressions." Science of People. December 14, 2016. Accessed March 31, 2017. http://www.scienceofpeople.com/2013/09/guide-reading-microexpressions/.
4. Ibid.
5. Scheve, Tom. "How many muscles does it take to smile?" HowStuffWorks Science. June 02, 2009. Accessed March 31, 2017. http://science.howstuffworks.com/life/inside-the-mind/emotions/muscles-smile.htm.
6. Morgan, Alice. *What Is Narrative Therapy: An Easy-to-Read Introduction.* Adelaide, Australia: Dulwich Centre Publications, 2002.
7. Cowman, L. B. *Streams in the Desert.* Grand Rapids, MI: Zondervan Pub. House, 1965, reprinted by permission.

Practice 2: *Welcome God into the Whys*

8. Kidd, Sue Monk. *When the Heart Waits: Spiritual Direction for Life's Sacred Questions.* San Francisco: HarperOne, 2006.
9. Medes, Lewis B. *Forgive and Forget: Healing the Hurts We Don't Deserve.* New York: HarperOne, 2007.
10. "Breathe." Dictionary.com. Accessed February 1, 2017. http://www.dictionary.com/browse/breathes.
11. "Composure." Dictionary.com. Accessed February 1, 2017. http://www.dictionary.com/browse/composure.
12. Frankl, Viktor. *Man's Search for Meaning.* Boston, MA: Beacon Press, 2006.
13. Welch, Edward T. *When People Are Big and God Is Small: Overcoming Peer Pressure.* Phillipsburg, NJ: Presbyterian and Reformed Publishing Company, 1997.
14. "Hold fast." Urbandictionary.com. Accessed February 8, 2017. http://www.urbandictionary.com/define.php?term=hold%20fast&defid=9523373.
15. "H3201–yakol–Strong's Hebrew Lexicon (KJV)." Blue Letter Bible. Accessed March 31, 2017. https://www.blueletterbible.org//lang/Lexicon/Lexicon.cfm?Strongs=H3201&t=KJV.
16. TEDxTalks. "TEDxSIT–Dr. Elke Rechberger–Listening between the Lines." YouTube. May 19, 2011. Accessed March 31, 2017. https://www.youtube.com/watch?v=dAoNhX54cAg.

17. Lu, Xin-An, and Hong Wang. *A Manual of Guidelines, Quotations, and Versatile Phrases for Basic Oral Communication*. New York: IUniverse, 2003.

18. "Elevate." Dictionary.com. Accessed February 16, 2017. http://www.dictionary.com /browse/elevate.

19. "The Heart of Innovation: 25 Quotes on the Power of Story." The Heart of Innovation: 25 Quotes on the Power of Story. Accessed March 11, 2017. http://www.ideachampions .com/weblogs/archives/2014/02/_the_world_is_n.shtml.

Practice 3: *Choose Healthy over Unhealthy*

20. "Viktor Frankl Quotes." The Ardent Axiom. July 16, 2011. Accessed February 17, 2017. https://merancis.com/quotes/viktor-frankl-quotes/.

21. "A quote from *The End of the Affair*." Goodreads. Accessed February 18, 2017. https:// www.goodreads.com/quotes/125911-a-story-has-no-beginning-or-end-arbitrarily -one-chooses.

22. "Bessel van der Kolk. Restoring the Body: Yoga, EMDR, and Treating Trauma." On Being. Accessed February 18, 2017. https://www.onbeing.org/programs/bessel -van-der-kolk-restoring-the-body-yoga-emdr-and-treating-trauma.

23. "Apr 29: Catherine of Siena (2): A saint for today." Catholicireland.net. Accessed February 20, 2017. https://www.catholicireland.net/saintoftheday/catherine-of -siena-a-saint-for-today/.

24. Shaia, Alexander J., and Michelle Gaugy. *The Hidden Power of the Gospels: Four Questions, Four Paths, One Journey*. New York: HarperOne, 2010.

25. "Whose Am I? or, Who am I? And How About Just Saying No . . ." Monkey Mind. October 26, 2011. Accessed March 31, 2017. http://www.patheos.com/blogs /monkeymind/2011/10/whose-am-i-or-who-am-i-and-how-about-just-saying-no.html.

26. "Identity." Dictionary.com. Accessed February 1, 2017. http://www.dictionary.com /browse/identity.

27. *American Heritage® Dictionary of the English Language, Fifth Edition*. S.v. "identity." Retrieved March 31, 2017 from http://www.thefreedictionary.com/identity.

28. *Webster's Dictionary 1828, Online Edition*. Webster's Dictionary 1828 "belong." Accessed March 31, 2017. http://webstersdictionary1828.com/Dictionary/belong.

29. Introduction to attachment theory in developmental psychology, including Bowlby and Ainsworth's contributions, evaluation, and criticisms of attachment theory. "How Your Infant Attachments Can Affect You in Later Life." *Psychologist World*. Accessed March 31, 2017. https://www.psychologistworld.com/developmental/attachment-theory.

30. "A quote from *This Is My Story*." Goodreads. Accessed March 31, 2017. https://www .goodreads.com/quotes/11035-no-one-can-make-you-feel-inferior-without-your-consent.

Practice 4: *Pray Through and Stay with the Process*

31. Lamott, Anne. *Operating Instructions: A Journal of My Son's First Year*. New York: Anchor Books, 2005.

32. "Meaner." Dictionary.com. *Dictionary.com Unabridged*. Random House, Inc. http:// www.dictionary.com/browse/meaner. Accessed March 1, 2017.

33. "Well meaning." Dictionary.com. *Dictionary.com Unabridged*. Random House, Inc. http://www.dictionary.com/browse/wellmeaning. Accessed March 1, 2017.

34. Goll, James W. "3 Stages of Prayer We Must Learn." *Charisma Magazine*. Accessed February 23, 2017. http://www.charismamag.com/spirit/prayer/17574-3-stages -of-prayer.

35. Ibid.

36. Lamott, Anne. *Plan B: Further Thoughts on Faith*. New York: Riverhead Books, 2006.

37. "Stay." Merriam-Webster.com. Accessed February 24, 2017. https://www.merriam -webster.com/dictionary/stay.

38. Ibid.

39. Wicks, Robert J. *Spiritual Resilience: 30 Days to Refresh Your Soul*. Cincinnati, OH: Franciscan Media, 2015.

40. Meyer, F. B. *Moses: the Journey of Faith*. Chattanooga, TN: AMG Publishers, 2001.

Practice 5: *Collect Strength*

41. Rilke, Rainer Maria. *Letters to a Young Poet*. New York: Penguin Books, 2016.

42. Cernovich, Mike. "Why One-in-Four Modern Women Have Mental Health Issues and Take Drugs." Mike Cernovich Presents Danger & Play. February 10, 2017. Accessed February 26, 2017. https://www.dangerandplay.com/2017/02/10/why-one-in-four -modern-women-have-mental-health-issues-and-take-drugs/.

43. "G373–anapauō–Strong's Greek Lexicon (KJV)." Blue Letter Bible. Accessed February 26, 2017. https://www.blueletterbible.org//lang/Lexicon/Lexicon. cfm?Strongs=G373&t=KJV.

44. "Permit." Merriam-Webster.com. Accessed February 26, 2017. https://www.merriam- webster.com/dictionary/permit.

45. Brown, Brené. *Rising Strong*. New York: Random House, 2017.

46. Lindbergh, Anne Morrow. *Gift from the Sea*. London: Chatto & Windus, 2015.

47. Ibid.

48. "Connect." Dictionary.com. *Dictionary.com Unabridged*. Random House, Inc. http:// www.dictionary.com/browse/connect. Accessed February 27, 2017.

49. "G26–agapē–Strong's Greek Lexicon (KJV)." Blue Letter Bible. Accessed March 31, 2017. https://www.blueletterbible.org//lang/Lexicon/Lexicon.cfm?Strongs=G26&t=KJV.

50. "Selfish." Merriam-Webster.com. Accessed April 1, 2017. https://www.merriam-webster .com/dictionary/selfish.

51. Lindbergh, Anne Morrow. *Gift from the Sea*. London: Chatto & Windus, 2015.

52. Ibid.

53. Ibid.

54. Silf, Margaret. *Inner Compass: An Invitation to Ignatian Spirituality*. Chicago: Loyola Press, 2007.

Practice 6: *Wait for the Peace that Passes Understanding*

55. Kidd, Sue Monk. *When the Heart Waits: Spiritual Direction for Life's Sacred Questions*. San Francisco: HarperOne, 2006.

56. Cowman, L. B. *Streams in the Desert*. Grand Rapids, MI: Zondervan Pub. House, 1965.

57. "Idealizing Intimacy." Focus on the Family. February 17, 2009. Accessed March 1, 2017. http://www.focusonthefamily.com/marriage/preparing-for-marriage/what-it-means-to -be-intimate/idealizing-intimacy.

58. Sorge, Bob. "Bob Sorge." bobsorge.com. March 07, 2014. Accessed March 2, 2017. http://bobsorge.com/2014/03/lessons-from-jacob-complete-series/.

59. "H6960–qavah–Strong's Hebrew Lexicon (KJV)." Blue Letter Bible. Accessed March 31, 2017. https://www.blueletterbible.org//lang/Lexicon/Lexicon.cfm?Strongs=H6960&t =KJV.

60. Lisitsa, Ellie. "The Positive Perspective: Dr. Gottman's Magic Ratio!" The Gottman Institute. February 12, 2017. Accessed March 3, 2017. https://www.gottman.com/blog /the-positive-perspective-dr-gottmans-magic-ratio/.

61. Tugend, Alina. "Praise Is Fleeting, but Brickbats We Recall." *The New York Times*. March 23, 2012. Accessed April 01, 2017. http://www.nytimes.com/2012/03/24/your-money /why-people-remember-negative-events-more-than-positive-ones.html.

62. Popova, Maria. "When Leaving Becomes Arriving: Poet and Philosopher David Whyte on Ending Relationships." Brain Pickings. September 21, 2015. Accessed January 15, 2017. https://www.brainpickings.org/2015/04/06/david-whyte-the-journey-house-of -belonging/. Used by permission.

Practice 7: *Embracing a Teachable Spirit*

63. "Ancora Imparo." Training for Warriors. January 29, 2016. Accessed February 2, 2017. http://www.trainingforwarriors.com/ancora-imparo/.

64. "Viktor Frankl Quotes." The Ardent Axiom. July 16, 2011. Accessed February 17, 2017. https://merancis.com/quotes/viktor-frankl-quotes/.

65. *American Heritage® Dictionary of the English Language, Fifth Edition*. S.v. "tipping point." Retrieved April 1, 2017 from http://www.thefreedictionary.com/tipping+point.

66. Rinehart, Paula. *Strong Women, Soft Hearts*. Nashville, TN: W Pub. Group, 2001.

67. Myss, Caroline. *Why People Don't Heal and How They Can*. North Sydney: Random House Australia, 2011.

68. "Oxford Dictionaries: Dictionary, Thesaurus, & Grammar." Oxford Dictionaries | English. Accessed April 01, 2017. https://en.oxforddictionaries.com/.

69. Frankel, Bruce. *What Should I Do with the Rest of My Life?: True Stories of Finding Success, Passion, and New Meaning in the Second Half of Life*. New York: Avery, 2011.

70. *American Heritage® Dictionary of the English Language, Fifth Edition*. S.v. "tough." Retrieved April 1 2017 from http://www.thefreedictionary.com/tough.

71. *American Heritage® Dictionary of the English Language, Fifth Edition*. S.v. "tender." Retrieved April 1 2017 from http://www.thefreedictionary.com/tender.

Practice 8: *Take the Leap and Trust Again*

72. "Erin Hanson Quotes (Author of *Reverie*)." Erin Hanson Quotes (Author of *Reverie*). Accessed March 20, 2017. https://www.goodreads.com/author/quotes/7802403. Erin_Hanson.

73. Rinehart, Paula. *Strong Women, Soft Hearts*. Nashville, TN: W Pub. Group, 2001.

74. *Webster's Dictionary 1828 Online Edition*. Webster's Dictionary 1828. Webster's Dictionary 1828 "trust." Accessed March 22, 2017. http://webstersdictionary1828.com/Dictionary/trust.

75. *Webster's Dictionary 1828 Online Edition*. Webster's Dictionary 1828. Webster's Dictionary 1828 "reliance." Accessed March 22, 2017. http://webstersdictionary1828.com/Dictionary/reliance.

76. *Webster's Dictionary 1828 Online Edition*. Webster's Dictionary 1828. Webster's Dictionary 1828 "veracity." Accessed March 22, 2017. http://webstersdictionary1828.com/Dictionary/veracity.

77. *Webster's Dictionary 1828 Online Edition*. Webster's Dictionary 1828. Webster's Dictionary 1828 "integrity." Accessed March 22, 2017. http://webstersdictionary1828.com/Dictionary/integrity.

78. "Depend." Dictionary.com. *Dictionary.com Unabridged*. Random House, Inc. http://www.dictionary.com/browse/depend. Accessed March 23, 2017.

79. Tozer, A. W. *Knowledge of the Holy: The Attributes of God*. North Fort Myers, FL: Faithful Life Publishers, 2014.

80. Ibid.

81. Ibid.

82. "Rigger's Pledge." Rigger's Pledge. Accessed March 28, 2017. http://www.parachuteservices.com/html/Other/riggers_pledge.html.

83. "US Army Airborne School." Baseops. Accessed March 28, 2017. http://www.baseops.net/basictraining/airborne.

84. "Rigger's Pledge." Rigger's Pledge. Accessed March 28, 2017. http://www.parachuteservices.com/html/Other/riggers_pledge.html.

85. Chambers, Oswald. *My Utmost for His Highest: The Classic Daily Devotional*. Uhrichsville, OH: Barbour Books, 2015.

86. "Introduction to Free Fall." The Physics Classroom. Accessed February 25, 2017. http://www.physicsclassroom.com/class/1Dkin/u1l5a.

87. "Gravity." Dictionary.com. *Dictionary.com Unabridged*. Random House, Inc. http://www.dictionary.com/browse/gravity. Accessed March 30, 2017.

88. "Panic Disorder." Psychology Today. May 08, 2017. Accessed September 05, 2017. https://www.psychologytoday.com/conditions/panic-disorder.

89. "G18–agathos–Strong's Greek Lexicon (KJV)." Blue Letter Bible. Accessed April 1, 2017. https://www.blueletterbible.org//lang/Lexicon/Lexicon.cfm?Strongs=G18&t=KJV

90. "G2853– kollaō–Strong's Greek Lexicon (KJV)." Blue Letter Bible. Accessed April 1, 2017. https://www.blueletterbible.org//lang/Lexicon/Lexicon.cfm?Strongs=G2853&t=KJV

Practice 9: *Smile at Your Future*

91. *The Emotionally Healthy Woman Workbook*. Zondervan. Accessed March 20, 2017. http://www.zondervan.com/the-emotionally-healthy-woman-workbook.

92. "Oprah Winfrey quotes." ThinkExist.com. Accessed April 01, 2017. http://thinkexist.com/quotation/i_am_where_i_am_because_of_the_bridges_that_i/339100.html.

93. "Bridge." Dictionary.com. *Dictionary.com Unabridged*. Random House, Inc. http://www.dictionary.com/browse/bridge. Accessed March 21, 2017.

94. *American Heritage® Dictionary of the English Language, Fifth Edition*. S.v. "swallow." Retrieved March 25, 2017, from http://www.thefreedictionary.com/swallow.

95. *American Heritage® Dictionary of the English Language, Fifth Edition*. S.v. "suppress." Retrieved March 25, 2017, from http://www.thefreedictionary.com/suppress.

96. Goleman, Daniel. "Health; New Studies Report Health Dangers of Repressing Emotional Turmoil." *The New York Times*. March 02, 1988. Accessed April 1, 2017. http://www.nytimes.com/1988/03/03/us/health-new-studies-report-health-dangers-of-repressing-emotional-turmoil.html.

97. Ibid.

98. "Don Henley Quotes." BrainyQuote. Accessed March 23, 2017. https://www.brainyquote.com/quotes/quotes/d/donhenley193059.html.

99. "A quote by Tim Duncan." Goodreads. Accessed February 23, 2017. https://www.goodreads.com/quotes/93387-good-better-best-never-let-it-rest-until-your-good.

100. "G2909–kreittōn–Strong's Greek Lexicon (KJV)." Blue Letter Bible. Accessed March 5, 2017. https://www.blueletterbible.org//lang/Lexicon/Lexicon.cfm?Strongs=G2909&t=KJV.

101. "G5236–hyperbolē–Strong's Greek Lexicon (KJV)." Blue Letter Bible. Accessed March 5, 2017. https://www.blueletterbible.org//lang/Lexicon/Lexicon.cfm?Strongs=G5236&t=KJV.

102. "G3598–hodos–Strong's Greek Lexicon (KJV)." Blue Letter Bible. Accessed March 5, 2017. https://www.blueletterbible.org//lang/Lexicon/Lexicon.cfm?Strongs=G3598&t=KJV.

103. *The Healing Power of Dialogue*. The Ikeda Center for Peace, Learning & Dialogue | Cambridge, MA. Accessed March 1, 2017. http://www.ikedacenter.org/thinkers-themes/themes/dialogue/yokota-on-dialogue.

104. *American Heritage® Dictionary of the English Language, Fifth Edition*. S.v. "footing." Retrieved April 1, 2017, from http://www.thefreedictionary.com/footing.

ACKNOWLEDGMENTS

To Andrea Alvord: From the moment I met you in the bathroom at church, I knew you were someone special. And then, a couple years later, we experienced Kenya together—amazing. We truly are "no longer slaves to sin . . . we are the children of God." Thank you for sitting with me in my "waiting room," and for our wonderful Wednesday chats. Cheers to more heartlifting travels in the future!

To Kristine Rand: You embody Ecclesiastes 4:10. I've lost count of all the times you've picked me up off the floor, both literally and emotionally. You are way more than a licensed social worker, my friend. You are a heartlifter whose presence radiates the love of Christ.

To Pastor Jim Wood: The moment I walked into First Hall, I felt right at home—a feeling I wasn't sure I'd ever feel again. But your powerful words and messages, along with your authentic friendship and spiritual direction, restored my faith in the power of a church community. As if that wasn't enough, I found a second home and church family in Kenya. I am so grateful.

To Pastor Valena Hoy: Dreaming alongside you has been powerful. Raising up a community of heartlifters, priceless. Thank you for listening between the lines of my endless musing and then carefully shaping it all into reality. You are truly remarkable.

To the women of Wednesday morning Bible study: Without a doubt, you helped me pray through and stay with the process of my long, dark valley through the shadow of waiting rooms. When women gather in the indomitable spirit of unity, miracles happen. First Peter 4:8 tells us to love one another deeply, and that is what you do!

To Will and Carrie (www.doebankdesigns.com), Kimberly (www.kimberlyroddy.com), and Tricia: Two words speak the loudest: thank you. Friends love at all times (Proverbs 17:17)—*all times*. Where would I be without your constant affirmation and words of support? Let's keep dreaming big!

To Pamela Clements, editor extraordinaire: When I first met you in Monterey, I knew instantly that you were special. You leaned in, listened closely, and genuinely cared about this "heartlift" idea spinning around in my head and heart. Your authenticity, passion, and publishing acumen bring light and love to this industry. I am blessed to have you as my editor and now, as friend.

To the remarkable Worthy Inspired team: Natalie Hanemann, Rachel Overton, Marilyn Jansen (editors); Melissa Reagan (creative director); Bruce Gore (cover designer); Bart Dawson (interior design); Ramona Wilkes (production). I kept pinching myself throughout this process as I felt I was living a dream. You all are indeed THE BEST! I owe you a big batch of my colossal chocolate chip cookies.

To Cat Hoort (Worthy Inspired Marketing): A little birdie told me you were truly remarkable, and she was right. You've brought Dr. Gottman's magical 5:1 ratio to life for me. For every negative interaction, it takes five positive interactions to restore emotional stability and security. Your affirming words about this project have heartlifted my creative confidence. Thank you.

To Terri Podlenski (Smart Creative Lab): Sometimes a vision takes time—a long time. Thank you for years of believing in my dream and for coming alongside to create artistic, effective graphics . . . on short notice, I add.

To the mamas of the Joy Village (Kenya): I knew when Kenya called, my life would never be the same. Sitting under a tin roof with torrential rain pouring around us, we opened God's Word. There were tears. Lots of laughter. Powerful prayers. Very fun Kenyan dancing and singing. And lifetime friendships formed. Your words of affirmation restored my value, worth, and dignity. Thank you from the bottom of my very blessed heart. (Learn more about these amazing women and Tree of Lives, a nonprofit I am blessed to be part of, at www.treeoflives.org.)

Finally, to the Heartlift Community: Look at what God has done! Thank you for always loving and supporting me and my insatiable passion for helping women become all God created them to be. Are you ready to roll up your sleeves and get to work? We have heartlifters to train! Stay tuned, the best is yet to come.

Join our community at

www.overcominghurtfulwords.com

to find incredible resources
and encouragement.

ABOUT THE AUTHOR

For more than twenty-five years, author Janell Rardon has spoken to thousands of women regionally, nationally, and internationally, welcoming women into a safe space where truth can be spoken and healing and hope can thrive—from local MOPS groups to international women's retreats.

After Janell's three children flew from the nest, she obtained her MA in Human Services Counseling (Marriage and Family Specialization) and board certification in Christian Life Coaching (AACC). She then opened her private practice, Heartlift Coaching & Consulting, in Virginia. Janell leans in and listens between the lines of women's stories every day, helping them overcome hurtful words and messages that hinder them from becoming the women God created them to be. Together, they reauthor new narratives filled with a deep sense of personal value, worth, and dignity, and move forward into lasting freedom in Christ.

Janell resides in Virginia with Rob, her husband of thirty-three years.

IF YOU ENJOYED THIS BOOK, WILL YOU CONSIDER SHARING THE MESSAGE WITH OTHERS?

Mention the book in a blog post or through Facebook, Twitter, Pinterest, or upload a picture through Instagram.

Recommend this book to those in your small group, book club, workplace, and classes.

Head over to facebook.com/worthypublishing, "LIKE" the page, and post a comment as to what you enjoyed the most.

Tweet "I recommend reading #OvercomingHurtfulWords by @Janell Rardon // @worthypub"

Pick up a copy for someone you know who would be challenged and encouraged by this message.

Write a book review online.

Visit us at worthypublishing.com

twitter.com/worthypub

instagram.com/worthypub

facebook.com/worthypublishing

youtube.com/worthypublishing